OUGHTEN HOUSE PUBLICATIONS

"Ascension Books for the Rising Planetary Consciousness"

Other Works by Eric Klein ⋄⋄⋄

The Crystal Stair: A Guide to the Ascension — A collection of channeled teachings received from Lord Sananda (Jesus) and other masters, describing the personal and planetary ascension process now occurring on our planet. The experience of ascension represents the next step of human evolution.

Ascension Tapes — A collection of channeled messages and meditation tapes, each bringing loving messages from the ascended masters.

THE INNER DOOR

CHANNELED DISCOURSES FROM
THE ASCENDED MASTERS ON
SELF-MASTERY AND ASCENSION

VOLUME ONE

BY

ERIC KLEIN

EDITED BY

SARA BENJAMIN

COVER DESIGN & ILLUSTRATION BY CATHIE BEACH
PUBLISHED BY OUGHTEN HOUSE PUBLICATIONS
LIVERMORE, CALIFORNIA, USA

THE INNER DOOR

CHANNELED DISCOURSES FROM THE ASCENDED
MASTERS ON SELF-MASTERY AND ASCENSION

VOLUME I

COPYRIGHT© 1993 BY ERIC KLEIN

FIRST EDITION

All rights reserved. No part of this book may be reproduced or transmitted or translated in any form or by any means, electronic or mechanical, including photocopying, recording, or by any information storage and retrieval system, except for inclusion of brief quotations in a review, without permission in writing from the publisher. This work is based upon channeled discourses from Sananda, Ashtar, Archangel Michael, St. Germain, and other ascended masters. The publisher and author are most willing to work with interested parties, provided that proper procedures are followed.

COVER DESIGN & ILLUSTRATION BY CATHIE BEACH

PUBLISHED BY

OUGHTEN HOUSE PUBLICATIONS
P.O. BOX 2008
LIVERMORE, CALIFORNIA, 94551-2008 USA
PRINTED BY DOUBLE EAGLE INDUSTRIES, BEN LOMOND, CALIFORNIA

Library of Congress Cataloging-in-Publication Data
Klein, Eric , 1951-
    The inner door : channeled discourses from the ascended masters on self-mastery and ascension / Eric Klein. -- 1st ed.
    p.   cm.
    ISBN 1-880666-03-0 : (v. 1 : pbk. : alk. paper) $14.50.
    ISBN 1-880666-16-2 (v. 2 : pbk. : alk. paper) : $14.50
    1. Spirit writings. 2. ascended masters. 3. Spirit life-
    Miscellanea. I. Title
    BF1290 K584   1993
    133.9' 1--dc20   93-29162
                                                 CIP
    ISBN 1-880666-03-0, Trade Publication
0 9 8 7 6 5 4 3 2 1

Printed in United States of America
Recycled and acid-free paper used.

DEDICATION ✦✦✦

For my fellow Lightworkers. May this work help to prepare us for wonders yet to come. And especially for all those who generously assisted us in our travels. Your love has proven we are a family.

ACKNOWLEDGMENT ✦✦✦

Undying gratitude to Jenny Annear, Robin Miner, Kara Alexander and Marie Damschen for the many self-less hours spent transcribing these channelings, to Sara Benjamin for supreme editing assistance, and to Robert Gerard for his great friendship and support through all lightstorms and transformations.

TABLE OF CONTENTS

PUBLISHER'S NOTE ✤✤✤

The channeled material presented in this book is a form of documentary concerning spiritual and psychological matters. It reflects transmitted information. The reader's interpretation of this or any other channeled information is subject to his or her ego and belief systems.

The language used in this book has been transcribed from the actual transmissions of the ascended masters with the least possible alteration in meaning. There are a few words which are used in unconventional ways, so that the essence of the channeled thought remains unchanged.

We at Oughten House extend our wholehearted appreciation and gratitude to each of our Literary Producers for making this publication possible: Marge and John Melanson, Barbara Rawles, Robin Drew, Irit Levy, Debbie Detwiler, Kiyo Monro, Alice Tang, Eugene P. Tang, Brad Clarke, Ruth Dutra, Nicole Christine, Dennis Donahue, Kathy Cook, Fred J. Tremblay, and Kimberley Mullen.

PREFACE

The channelings included in these books were selected from well over 100 sessions recorded between the summer of 1990 and autumn of 1992. With so many discourses to choose from, it has been quite a challenge deciding which to include. In fact, the quantity of channelings that do seem necessary has caused us to put this work out in two volumes. My hope is that these messages, in combination with those included in *The Crystal Stair*, will form a fairly complete presentation of the information and training we are receiving.

One further note concerning these books: each chapter is an individual class or "energetic training session." To receive the maximum enjoyment and "activation," I recommend taking a few moments to request the presence of the teacher(s) presenting the discourse, prior to diving in. There are wonderful healing and transformational energies contained within each chapter, and the masters have promised to honor all requests for their assistance as we work with this material.

So, best wishes to all who find their paths winding through these pages. It has been an honor to participate in this sacred work.

Eric Klein
Santa Cruz, California

INTRODUCTION

SANANDA

Greetings, dear brothers and sisters. It is with great joy in our hearts that we bring you these channeled discourses. As you are aware, planet Earth is experiencing great stirrings, not the least of which is the quickening now occurring within human consciousness. With each passing hour the planetary ascension process moves forward, carrying all beings nearer to the completion we have long awaited.

Perhaps it would be pertinent to state, in this introduction, how very important it is becoming for each of you to learn to follow the guidance and direction you receive through the channel of your own hearts. All teachings serve only as signposts created by those who have gone before, pointing the way toward a mastery each student must achieve in their own unique way. We are here to share a higher awareness that exists, to show you that God-realization and ascension are passages you are destined to walk through on your evolutionary journey. The concepts and perspectives you may choose in attempting to understand this process are of little concern to us. Your practical attainment remains our primary focus.

Many masters have given of their love and wisdom in the creation of these volumes. We ask only that you open your hearts and minds to the energies transmitted through these words and through our beings as you receive them. God is love and light. You are love and light. Receive and share. There are no limits. We are with you. Walk through the door.

ONE

The Inner Door

SANANDA

Good day, my fellow travelers. This is Sananda here with you. A long journey it has been, and yet the adventure has just begun. I thank you this day for your attendance here. I thank you for the efforts you have made individually, and as groups. For the work that you do together is not only for yourselves but for all — for all of this world, which does need so much lifting, which can benefit so much from this heart energy that we share.

In your path, in your moment to moment experience, there are many levels of awareness. And available to your consciousness simultaneously are many dimensions of experience for you to feel, for you to merge with and share. In your efforts, your meditation practices, and all of the means you use to connect with Spirit, you are offering yourself to be utilized as a channel to bring these higher-dimensional energies through.

You are asking your spirit to open doors within yourself that have been closed, doors that lead to higher-dimensional awareness. Today I would like to speak about the energy of love, surrender, and devotion, the energy you might call your heart energy, and its role in opening these inner doors. I know you have been here for a full afternoon. I will not speak for a very long time, but I do ask you to focus yourselves and relax and breathe with me, for I also would like to perform some healing work with you. Your ability to experience the benefits of this healing are dependent only upon your ability to open your hearts and to feel, to let go.

A human being is a multi-dimensional manifestation. A human being is a doorway, a bridge between the physical world and the spiritual worlds, of which there are many. The goal of Light Workers, the goal of the ascending human being, is to cross that bridge and to reconnect consciously with the higher-dimensional Self that you are. This is something that is accomplished only through the opening of the heart. Simply knowing that there is a higher-dimensional aspect of yourself is a good beginning, but it does not allow you access to that bridge, to that inner door. Though a being might be very wise philosophically, intellectually, they are no closer to the ascension than a being who is in ignorance if the heart is not open, if the practical experience of spirituality is missing. This is where your commitment comes in, where your spiritual practice comes in. And most of you understand what I mean when I say "opening the heart." Some of you have more work to do in this area. I will assist you. You need to love yourselves as I love you. You need to give yourselves, as I have given myself to you, so that we can connect, so that I can come through you in this moment and unlock the inner door and grant you access to that inner bridge. It is necessary on this path to integrate the intellectual knowledge, practical experience, emotional experience, to integrate and balance all that you have received of guidance — and the point of balance is the heart. The heart is your center of discernment. From that center of love within you, you are integrated and balanced to make whatever adjustments are required in your life, to assist you in the opening that is required. For what I am speaking of is truly a physical and a spiritual experience.

On your path, dear ones, you must listen to the subtle guidance you receive: from your physical bodies, from your emotional bodies, from your higher Self, and from the many masters and angels that work with you. The heart is the spiritual center of the human being. Though you might receive information through your higher centers — in telepathic communications, for example — only in moving this information through the heart center does it have any real meaning for you. Then it will affect the physical and the emotional self, the human self that is calling out for assistance. The I AM presence is perfectly adept just as it is. It is the human self that is crying out for love. And it is the human self that must walk through the inner door of the heart, there to be greeted by the Christ, as I am the shepherd destined to guide you. I don't care if you know that it is I who fills you with love, but I do care that you are filled with love. It is my duty to melt your hearts, dear ones, to help you to access your innate innocence and purity. It is there, and you have never left it but only in your sophistications, and in your fears, and in your belief systems of lack and limitation.

The opening of the heart center grants a special grace and presence and healing. And in this moment you may be able to feel my energies penetrating you in a healing way, filling your bodies. There is much more occurring here than meets the eye or the ear. If your heart centers are open, you can feel it. If your heart centers require more opening, I am working in that way. You have total freedom, my dear ones — freedom of manifestation, freedom of choice — and it is my pleasure and the pleasure of the Creator to watch you and to experience with you as you enjoy your freedom of manifestation. But it is also our duty to assist you in accessing the free choice to return to Source in a practical and real way, in a way that you have called ascension. And this can only be accomplished through giving yourself to Spirit and in allowing the heart opening.

You see, we don't care what you are thinking about in your philosophies, or what perspective you choose to engage in with regards to the ascension. But it is very important to us that you experience ascension, as it is your next step. It is very important to us. It does not matter to me the many ways human beings have referred to me or thought about me or not thought about me, as I am secure in my station. And yet it is necessary for all beings desiring to grow to pass through the inner door that I create within you, that I co-create with your acquiescence. I may surprise you from time to time. Just as you think you might know me, perhaps I might reveal to you more of myself, another aspect of my nature, as I reveal that it is another aspect of your nature as well.

For we are in relationship, and I am fully committed to this long term relationship. And for those of you who know you are in love, your hearts are mine — mine to enjoy, mine to share, as my heart is yours. It is not necessary for beings of this planet to ever think of the word Jesus, the word Sananda, the word Michael, or any of the other ways human beings have referred to me. I have no interest in creating a fan club. Yet I have an interest in you and in the opening of your hearts, and we do have a relationship. You will understand the nature of it as you progress more and more, as all beings in this local universe are my responsibility, are my co-creations. Therefore I am the shepherd, and you are aspects of a certain flock that you could say is winding its way back to Source. And as you attain to your ascension, you too will become shepherds of this flock, and neither will you care how others refer to you. You will only care that they do open their hearts with sincerity and allow the magic to take place. Magic is another way of describing grace, as one of you has asked the question, "What is grace?" Grace, in one sense, is a magical transformation that affects a human being, that allows the higher Self to be totally integrated in the physical form in the experience of God-realization, which opens the door to ascension, the actual lifting into immortality.

So, we could sit here and speak about the countless universes and the spiritual hierarchies that serve in many capacities, and yet the critical experience for you at this time is this heart opening, this opening to your spiritual Self, the practical experience. Then you can walk among the hierarchy yourselves and formulate your own opinions. What do you think of St. Germain? You have a certain experience of him now perhaps. When you walk side by side and converse with him in the higher dimensions, you can formulate your own opinions, as he reveals his nature to you more fully. And this is what we are getting at. This is what we are here to achieve, dear ones — the practical experience, so that you can fully share that which we enjoy in abundance: love, light, wisdom, a more cosmic awareness.

In my experience as Jesus (which was some time ago, but to me not that long ago), I had many experiences in physical form, just as you are having. And toward the conclusion of my Earth life, I spent a great deal of time in conversing and sharing from my heart in teaching the truths that I had experienced. And there were many, many beings that would come and listen. And as I spoke to them in simple language that they could understand, all the while I was working with the heart center, opening those beings just as we do this day. You have come a long way in your understanding, in your sophistication, and yet a very short way compared to where your destination leads you. And still I work with you in my simple way, to open your hearts, to open the doorway within you, that you might access all that you are and receive the answers for yourselves. That is the only way they will be real to you.

Wisdom, dear ones, is experience. Knowledge is not wisdom until it is applied experientially. The universe as it exists is composed of many dimensions, and many, many manifestations within these. From a third-dimensional platform it is all but impossible to get a true glimpse of what's really going on. You can receive great infusions of love and light direct from Source, for you are never separate, yet there is a veiling that is necessary for your own safety, for your own learning and your ability to function here. This is why we are so adamant about inspiring you upon the ascension path. For whatever you might study here, the highest study is in your own heart. The highest practice is surrender to Spirit, opening to your innocence, your purity. In my Earth teachings, many beings would long for me to speak to them of higher things — the astrologers and the Magi — and of course at times I would share with them to the level of their ability to comprehend. Yet always my work was in the heart — always working to open and to align all of the spiritual bodies, to merge the physical with the spiritual. And this we do today. And this you do today in sharing these energies with your fellow humans as I share with you.

There is no higher experience than love. If you think you have experienced love, you haven't seen anything yet. You can talk about it as if you know what it is, and to a degree you do, but always know that it is an infinite resource. And this love is as close as you will come to understanding and being one with me, to understanding the Source of all that is. I honor you, dear ones, for your commitment, for your openness, for the love that I do feel in your presence. It is truly inspiring to me. As Ashtar said, it is a family reunion, so we can get a little bit mushy. I would like to share with you that there is no separation between us. In the moment that you think of me, or call upon me for assistance, I am there and holding you in my arms. And no matter how great a master you become, my arms will be always able to enfold you, and you will always have an experience of innocence in my company. Though I will speak to you as an equal and honor you as a master, in your heart there is an aspect of the being that you are that is as a child to me. And I am the father to that child.

Truly, if you would have in your heart a desire to know, for example, what happened two thousand years ago, what it was like, I could talk about it from my perspective. But that would not be yours. I would rather open your heart and give you access to your spirit, so that you can find out for yourself. For this is a greater service to you. So you see, perhaps I am here to trick you a little bit. I tell you about the wonderful universes that exist, the fields of energy, the fields of experience that are for you — but only enough to whet your appetite — for I seek to inspire you to take those steps, to experience those practically for yourselves. No matter what perspectives you hold, no matter who you are, whatever your personal experience is or has been, you have one thing in common: if you desire to experience your ascension, if you desire a higher perspective, if you desire to roam the galaxies as an immortal being, you will have to walk through the doorway of your hearts. And as you do I will be there with you, holding your hands, enfolding you with my love, encouraging you, perhaps telling you a few jokes on the way — whatever is necessary to enhance your trust, to enhance your innocence, to give you the ability to relax and surrender. For this is a path of surrender. Ultimately you have to let go of everything. And only Spirit is there to guide you along, to pull you along. Many of you know what I am speaking of, as you have had to relinquish attachments in this world. You have been shown them and shown how they hold you back. So all attachment will be surrendered, and as you give yourself to Spirit with commitment it will be accomplished gracefully and with relative ease. This option is open to all human beings, the same path that you walk. I don't care what religion you might refer to yourself as, you will walk through the same doorway. Wouldn't you think it wise to become acquainted with that doorway directly? And this is what we are doing with you in your lives, and in this moment that we share.

So breathe with me and access that heart energy. The breath meditation that we have recommended is a meditation that I taught when I was in physical body. The light meditation is the same as taught by all the many masters who have been here. This transmission has been given, the information concerning the breath and the light, the celestial harmonies within, and many techniques have been shared. Many have shared these simple techniques. And you carry this breath with you always. It is the key that unlocks your heart, allowing the light to penetrate into the physical, into all of the cells of your body for healing, for upliftment, for the shift that needs to take place. You've got to bring this body with you, you see. And this lifting of your energies — this work is your walk down the aisle, you could say, in the ceremony. And as you have walked and completed that little stroll, that little energy lifting, you are prepared for the marriage ceremony. So the breath and the light are key for you, dear ones. Give yourself to that. Give yourself to meditation practice and experience what you are and what I am. What is our relationship? What does exist beyond the realm of the mind and the ideas, the emotions, the physical? All these are sacred, and yet to experience them as sacred, you must experience the divine higher Self. And this is done in a practical way, through surrendering and following the guidance you receive through your heart centers.

If you have questions of discernment, how will you answer them? If your heart is open, you will have no problem with discernment. Of the many teachings, the many channels, the many books that you can read now, how will you know what is for you? How will you know what is a true perspective that can benefit you, or what is extraneous to your process? If your heart is open, you will take what you receive and bring it through the heart — for the heart knows what is truth. The heart will resonate or not resonate with that information, that teaching, that energy, and it will be easy for you. And then, as Ashtar has suggested, trust. Trust that you can rely upon your heart to tell you. If you are unclear, do not be concerned. Just give yourself more to the practice of meditation and allow me to open your heart. I will share with you in ways that will very quickly open you to total discernment. And your discernment, dear ones, is for you alone. It is not for you to judge or criticize the paths others may take, but only to know what is *your* path. And this path is a moment to moment experience.

So the choice is yours, dear ones. Your free will choice, as to your alignment, your perspectives, as to whether you choose to attend to that which I have been speaking of this day. Again — you are sovereign beings. I only ask you to, with humility, open your hearts and consider my words. Consider the possibility that I am Sananda, that I am in love with you, that I can assist in your ascension. Open yourself to the possibility that we are lovers, and see what happens. This is all I ask. Your hearts have an automatic pilot. When they feel love they know what to do — and it only takes a moment. One moment of true love and you're in love forever. Then you can't settle for anything less. And I ask you not to settle for anything less. Your time, your energy are precious. Spend them in ways that are meaningful to you. Spend them in ways that are nurturing and healing to you. And don't worry about what others think — only be concerned with what you experience within yourself.

So, we could sit like this for hours, but I think you might become bored with me, for it has been a long day. I would like to share that the energy work that we have done with you this day has been very effective. And you will realize — if not in this moment, later this day, later this week, at some point in your life — that something has occurred this day that was very precious. And I hope you will think of me when that realization dawns upon you. I hope it will cause within you a feeling of devotion and love, and that you will give that love back to Source and allow yourselves to be used as channels to assist in the upliftment of this world, and whatever worlds might follow. Once you are immortal, you know, you're not on any schedules. Schedules are the result of death. Death is the cause of all of your worrying about time. When there is no more death you can take your time or run as fast as you want.

So, I love you so much, dearest ones. Breathe with me just for a moment. I know you have given yourselves with focus this day, but I ask just for a moment more of your time. Know that you are surrounded in a beautiful energy field, an aspect of myself, my presence. Know that you and I are united in love, in harmony, and that you can count upon these energies to assist you always. As you breathe, just feel the presence and allow this love energy to expand from this circle outwards in all directions. And let this be a healing for planet Earth.

So, dear ones, I bless you. I love you. I thank you again. I honor you for your commitment in being with us this day. Know this work is permanently sealed. Know the seeds that we have planted this day, if they do not blossom forth immediately, with your kind attention and focus will blossom forth most profoundly. Know these energies will assist in the healing of your physical bodies and in the integration of the spiritual Self with the physical, emotional, and mental bodies. Know that you are masters. If you were not masters you would not be here this day. And allow yourselves the nurturance that you desire and require. Listen to the needs of your bodies. Attend to this. Attend to the needs of your emotional bodies. Attend to the call of your hearts. Go within, into the spiritual Self, and all of these will balance and harmonize in your ascension. Your victory will be very glorious to perceive. So, I love you all so much. I will be with you as you desire. Good day.

∽ TWO ∽

State of the Mission

ASHTAR AND SANANDA

Good evening, my loved ones. This is your old friend Ashtar, piercing the veil of illusion to reach you and to share with you of my presence. I ask that you relax yourselves and be natural. We have some work to do this evening. We need to do some clearing, I can see. There are a lot of random thought patterns this evening. A lot emotional clearing is taking place. We will address this. I would like you to know that I am not alone this evening. Lord Sananda is also with us to lend his support and to assist us in our endeavors.

Simply to be embodied at this time on the Earth's surface is quite a challenge. And on top of that we are asking you to unfold your Earth missions and do more than simply survive. We are challenging you to complete your Earth missions and your service, to open to that which you are, the deeper levels of yourselves. So

I ask that you relax and breathe with me. I think you are going to enjoy this evening.

I would like to speak about the state of the mission. I will give you my "State of The Mission Address." I come to speak to you, my Earthly constituents, this evening. As you know we are having quite a campaign. At times it looks as if the opposition has us bamboozled. But we are not prepared to throw in the towel as of yet. You could say we have a few tricks up our sleeves. There is a great activation that is occurring now. We have spoken many times in the past about the waves of energy and about the various intensifications of spiritual grace and presence, and this process does continue. Perhaps you have been feeling a great clearing taking place within you in recent days and weeks. This is as a precursor to the new energies that are coming through and will be coming through more. There is another activation taking place through which we hope to awaken as many Starseeds and Light Workers as possible. And by awakening, I mean not merely opening your eyes, but actually getting out of bed! You know who you are. Actually getting up and moving around and beginning your daily responsibilities often takes a bit of initial effort. Some of you may be feeling that sense of drowsiness, that longing to remain in that comfortable nest of sleep. Nevertheless, we are here to rattle your cages and shake you and wake you. We are going to open the curtain and allow the sun to stream in upon you. If you can cooperate with these energies and open to them, we will not have to throw cold water on you.

So truly you are in the beginning stages of another great phase of awakening. The effects of these energies upon you will vary depending upon your alignment with your higher Selves and your Earth missions. If you are one who is in alignment and following your spiritual path then you will enjoy this as another wave of energy. It could be a little bit challenging. But nevertheless you will be able to enjoy it. If you are as ones who have been slumbering, these energies will call you to more self-examination. They will call you to view your lives from a higher perspective, and hopefully to inspire you to get on with your work — to get on with your mission, and the unfoldment of your own ascension and that of the planet's, which is the campaign we are all engaged in. It is time for each of you to come to grips with the challenge of who you are and what you are here to do, as you find it increasingly difficult to pull the covers over your head and remain simply a physical, mental, and emotional being. You are "in between a rock and a hard place," you could say. On one hand, you are opening to Spirit, but perhaps Spirit is coming through you more powerfully than you have imagined and calling you to unfold the magnificence of who you are. There is very little middle ground for those of you who are volunteers. Those of you who volunteered to come to this Earth plane many thousands of years ago to assist with the transformation that is now taking place, are under contract. This contract is calling you now to make a total commitment to your own enlightenment, your own ascension, and to following your spirit without hesitation in each moment of your lives.

Each of you have your own areas of expertise, your own ways of being. You each have various potentials within you. These are being tapped. If you have been feeling restless lately, perhaps you have been releasing those very patterns and limitations that will be needing to be out of the way. Those are things that have been clouding your judgment and your vision. I believe most of you have the vision to see the situation that planet Earth is in, that truly what is going to happen is going to happen very soon and very quickly. And you are being called to participate in this as channels of higher-dimensional energy, as channels of your own God-self and perhaps as channels of us, your compatriots of higher dimensions. It is not recommended that you continue to resist these energies if you have been. It is recommended that you go with the flow of these energies. They will become more and more powerful. If you are aligned with them you will become more and more powerful, more and more liberated, more in joy and love, and more able to function as a divine being, as the masters that you are. Resistance to these energies will only cause you difficulty and confusion. Perhaps you have had the experience of feeling called by your spirit, by your heart, by your guidance into particular ways of acting or being and you have pulled the covers over your heads and said, "No thank you. I think that sounds too difficult." And you try to go back to sleep. This is a common occurrence. You have all experienced it. What are the results of this resistance and this attempt to hide from your own Self? It generally results in less than perfect results, to put it mildly. It can result in physical or emotional discomforts, or any number of physical manifestations, even into manifesting strange occurrences and relationship experiences. Spirit is not playing around with any of you. You could say that Spirit is playing hardball at this time. As the campaign draws to a close we have got to pull out all the stops, you see. The laws that are in effect and are affecting you are immutable. It is all designed to assist in your ascension and in the release of all limitations and in the completion of your contracts. You have contracts that you have signed, that have been notarized. You can't get out of them. Sananda is quite a legal mind, did you know that? And he is holding your contracts within his heart.

On the other hand, if you are giving yourself to Spirit and doing your utmost to follow your guidance, your lives are becoming more and more wonderful. Your resistance is becoming less and less. Your fears are diminishing. You are realizing yourself not only as a third- and fourth-dimensional physical, emotional and mental being, but also as a higher-dimensional being. Your fifth-dimensional selves are connecting with you and you are feeling that presence and that power that is able to flow through your open channels. You are utilizing this energy to create and co-create the beautiful experience of service and of life for yourself and for others. I ask you to hear me this evening. I ask you to choose to follow Spirit at this time. It is challenging but it is the only way for you. There has been much talk about the comfort zone. It is a common expression that you use. Everyone says, "Well they are stuck in a comfort zone. They aren't into growing very quickly. They are enjoying their comfort zone." Well, we are creating a new comfort zone for all of you. It is a comfort zone that you will experience as you give yourselves to Spirit and as you experience your own ascension and the gradual lifting of your consciousness and your physical self into the higher dimensions. It will become more comfortable for you to follow this path than to resist. So how is that for a comfort zone!

So this activation, this energy that I am speaking of, is in its initial phases and will continue for some time. This may be a bit of a challenge for you at first, but the result of it inevitably will be that you are in the clear, that you become fully activated. The cobwebs of illusion and confusion will fall from your consciousness. It will become easier for you to master your ascension path, to master this third-dimensional stage of activity to the point where you are fully functioning as masters on the Earth plane.

In your self-examination, I must point out to you the importance of self love and self acceptance. You may look at yourselves and see the places where you have tried to pull the covers over your head, where you have resistance, and you may start whipping yourselves and think what a bad person you are. You may feel that you are not fulfilling your Earth mission. At that point and prior to that point I wish you to open to self love and acceptance. You need to be clear about what you are doing and why you are doing it. But you do not need to criticize yourselves. You may need to make adjustments in your lives and in your spiritual practices. These adjustments will be made more clear to you. For some of you it is only a very small amount of fine tuning. For others it might be a radical shift in your lifestyle and behavior. Sananda and the Heavenly

Father love you so much. Every possible grace is being offered to assist you to gain that clarity and that personal empowerment you require to continue, to unfold your missions in these troubled times on this world.

The energies of this world have become more and more chaotic and troubled because of the great clearings that are taking place. It requires you to be that much more focused. It requires you to remember with that much more clarity who you are and what you are here to do and to actually do that. Your intention is all important. Some of you are probably thinking that it is impossible and you will never be able to focus yourself and attain your ascension. You may feel it is too difficult. It is really not difficult. It is quite easy. If your intention is clear you will receive the guidance you need. And in receiving your guidance it is a choice, a simple choice in each moment whether or not to meditate. You are all faced with the choice daily whether to be conscious of your aliveness or whether to give yourself to external stimulation, of which there is much. It is very simple and it all occurs in the moment that you find yourselves in. It is never something that you have to do in the future. You may think that if you follow your mission you will have to do this or that or become a world teacher and may feel that it is all too frightening. And you may want to pull the covers over your head. But you see, that is a trick of your mind. Truly your mission is only in each moment and you will never be asked to perform or to open in any way that is not perfectly in alignment with who you are and what you are here to do.

Your joy is what we are here to uncover, you know. Your joy is aligned and directly connected with your mission. You know the New Age expression, "Do what you love and the money will follow." So do what you love. That is what you are here to do. You can spend hours and hours worrying about manifesting a sufficient financial situation to survive here, or you could just do what you love and trust. And if you don't know what you love, you can go inside and ask for guidance and do what occurs to you in that moment. The unfoldment and activation that we are speaking of is a moment-to-moment experience of following your feelings and your heart, and acting upon those impulses that you feel from within rather than reacting to external impulses. The external impulses that are available to you at this time to draw upon can be sheer lunacy. The thought patterns that are out there for you to draw upon are not entirely healthy for you. The thought patterns and programming that you have experienced in your lives and that are active now in the world are counter-productive to the ascension path. All the fears and worries and negative programming are all based upon the belief that you are poor, pitiful mortals, trapped in a body, struggling to survive in third-dimensional reality. You see, the very foundation of belief that this world has used to attempt to program human beings is based on illusion. You are immortal beings. You are powerful beings. There is nothing that can stop you in your activation and in attaining your complete ascension in this lifetime.

So, concerning the state of the mission, things are proceeding quite well. On a planetary scale the maelstrom of emotions and experiences that are present are being cleared. If you are feeling these types of experiences within you, or strange manifestations in your life, know that they are being cleared so that you can come into that state of full activation and empowerment. It seems to us that the number one challenge before the Starseeds is to remain awake. It is quite simple to feel that awakening when you first hear of the ascension plan. It is very easy to become excited about it and give yourself to that. But it seems from our observations that *maintaining* that awakened state is the challenge. Maintaining your focus and your trust and faith is the challenge for as long as it takes you to complete your missions. Fortunately for you, you are not alone. You have many guides and masters surrounding you and serving you with their grace and protection. Fortunately, it is not a matter of time but a matter of enlightenment and evolvement. We have been bringing through information to assist in your understanding of the ascension and evacuation plan and to assist in your awareness of what is occurring within you.

It does appear at this time that there will be several waves of mass ascension. I would say that the first and second waves of this experience will truly be a spiritual experience, and not evacuation in a merely physical sense. Some of you have listened to the tapes of our discussions of this. Some of you have not. As I said, we are making the rounds of our constituents. So, to make your leap into the ascended state is an experience of your own spiritual evolvement, achieved by giving yourself to meditation and following your guidance. I am asking that you not be attached to timetables or to any other manifestations or projection of times and dates, but I would say to attend to your spiritual growth. Attend to those energies that you are feeling in each moment. For you never know when it will occur with you. It may be that some will go into their full attainment of ascension earlier than others. The waves that we are speaking of will be energy waves. These energy waves will activate mass ascensions. It will be as a final nudge or a final energetic push for those who are at the threshold of the ascension experience. Your work is to prepare yourselves and maintain yourself at that threshold as best you can and to do what occurs to you in the meantime regarding activities of service and self-expression.

So we are asking you to understand a bit more about your ascension paths, to take the time to explore this and to give yourselves to it if it is your desire. There is so much more to experience. There is so much joy that awaits you. We call to you to give yourselves whole-heartedly to these awakenings and to your meditations. Have the awareness of the times you are living in. Do not take your reality from the television set or from the newspaper. Take your reality from us and from that which you perceive internally in your meditations. Listen to what your guides are telling you. Ordinary consciousness will tell you that nothing is happening, that the world is going along as usual, and that everything is under control. It will tell you that the world's problems can all be solved if we simply apply ourselves to them, because the alternative is impossible to imagine. The alternative you hold within your consciousness about planetary ascension, that you nurture with your spiritual work, is the alternative that will manifest.

So how do you like my campaign speech so far? There is more that we will do this evening but now is a good time to ask if any of you have questions for me.

"Did I understand that if we give ourselves diligently to meditation and spiritual growth that our veils could be lifted and we could manifest more effectively while we are still here on Earth?"

Yes, this is ultimately your path. You do not need to wait for any particular ascension experience, or the completion of that, before you can manifest the powers that you have within you. They will gradually manifest as you evolve and express. It is our intention to take each of you, with your willingness and assistance, into a place where you are able to manifest that which you require, where you are empowered sufficiently, where you are above the fray, liberated from emotional traumas and all of the dense energies that are still to be released here even while you are in your physical form. It is a process of unveiling, a process by which you remember who you are, and a process where you realize that you simply project thought and energy to manifest. The energies that are coming through now in these activations are going to result in your ability to manifest more powerfully. In fact, what you have been seeing around you are your creations. Part of self-

mastery and aligning with Spirit involves creating only
that which you truly want from your hearts, not that
which you are afraid of or are projecting out of fear or
other limitation. So manifestation is going to be intensified. That is why we say if you are giving yourself to
alignment with your spirit you will be manifesting
much more easily. If you are not, it will be more difficult. We're shaking the fence now, you see. Or rather,
the Heavenly Father is shaking the fence and we are
assisting. We are trying to nudge you to fall off on the
side of the light, to jump off into the light. It's not going
to be dull, my friends. Believe it or not, you are all very
brave individuals. You are most adventurous souls to
partake of this experiment. And truly it has been an
experiment. And we see it as successful.

*"Could you give me some help in differentiating
between when I am following my spiritual Self
and when I'm following my ego-self? I get very
confused about this and my fears get in the way.
I'm just not sure when I'm following my spirit."*

That is an excellent question. The result of this
activation, if you are applying yourself to meditation,
will be such that it will be much easier to distinguish.
The energies of Spirit will be felt more in a light and
harmonious fashion. The energies of the ego will be felt
in a heavier, denser, or more fearful fashion. Your discrimination will increase. My main advice is for you to

meditate. Give yourself fully to that, and pay attention to when you are acting and when you are reacting.

There will always be challenges to the unfoldment of your mission and to the following of your guidance. You might receive a very clear and powerful transmission in meditation guiding you in a certain avenue of activity. And at a certain point in that avenue of activity, you might encounter a challenge or a resistance, either externally or internally. Either way it is the same. The resistance is a manifestation of your inner resistance. It is a test and a strengthening for you to see if you will follow through. So it is not always a bed of roses. There are always tests, trials, and challenges. What will generally happen is when those challenges arise, that is where your limited ego-self will try to convince you that you aren't following Spirit because the path is difficult. It will try to convince you that you've gotten off the path somehow or you wouldn't be feeling the resistance or the challenge. You'd think it should be easy to follow Spirit. It can be a very tricky situation. I would say to dive into meditation and that will sharpen your discrimination, and pray for guidance and assistance. Be conscious of your choices. Over time this will be made more and more clear. Trial and error sometimes is necessary. At first your expressions and your guidance will be received very enthusiastically and joyfully. Later on you might think about it and your ego will come in and say, "That's impossible. I could never do that," or it will create fear around that expression.

So following your initial impulse through the fear and resistance is what strengthens you. When you can walk through fear realizing that it is just a shadow, at that point a broad horizon opens before you. Your vision becomes more long-range. If you are always afraid to walk through that shadow of fear, through that veil, your sight will be more shortsighted and you will always be limiting yourselves. It is only a matter of walking through that shadow a few times before you realize it for what it is and then you take your power and you begin to live as the master that you are. When you don't feel clear, meditate.

"When you talked about the first wave of ascension being an energy wave and that we will still be walking the Earth as ascended beings, will our missions change when we finally achieve that ascended state?"

This is not quite what I am trying to say. What I am saying is not that you will continue to walk the Earth in your usual fashion. You will go into the higher dimensions. You will be lifted. You will probably find yourselves surrounded by those of the Ashtar Command. But it will be an experience of ascension, not merely of evacuation. You will not be taken up into a spaceship and worked with further until you are able to ascend. That will be for the last wave. When actual ascension occurs, you merge into the higher dimensions. It may appear to others that you have disappeared, or it may appear that you were lifted and dissolved into light. After this experience you may have a bit of a break before you resume Earth activities. But at that point when you resume your Earth activities you will not be in a physical body, you will be in a light body. All of your powers and mastery will be fully manifested.

"Is a similar thing going to happen to members of the animal kingdom? Will the animals also ascend?"

Yes, something like that. The animals cannot attain ascension as human beings can, but they can be lifted in the final evacuation waves into the ships to be re-populated into the Earth plane when the Earth is cleared and returned to its pristine condition. They will be harmonized. They will not be ascended but they will be in their true states. Even the animal kingdom has been quite upset by the negativity that has been mani-fested on the Earth plane. Some of the more ferocious beasts were not originally that way. They have been learning from human beings. Some of them are quite upset about the state of affairs and do not wish to return to Earth. It will be very Eden-like. It will be a part of the completion of the Earth's ascension process.

❦

This is Sananda. Greetings. I trusted you wouldn't mind me interrupting your meditation. I come but briefly to share my love and to bless you all this evening — and to ask you for your vote! Sananda for President — Ashtar for Vice President!

There is truly a great deal occurring as Ashtar has said. The activation that is taking place now will continue for some time, perhaps months. It is time for you to re-focus yourselves and recommit yourselves. The love that is awaiting is here now, within you. The power you are waiting to manifest is here now, within you. There is no more need to wait. If you have been one who has waited all of your life to know why you are here and what you are supposed to do, who you are — well, that time is here. We work with you so closely. We surround you and overshadow you with our guidance. The planet is in a critical state and now I ask each of you volunteers to give yourselves wholeheartedly to the completion of your missions. And this of course begins with your own ascension and with your giving of yourself to Spirit and channeling through the energies that we desire to bring through to the Earth plane. You are our hands and our feet. You are the vehicles through which we channel our love. You will be strengthened. You will be armored in my love and in my light, for the days ahead. You will witness many transformations. We ask you to maintain contact with your higher Self and not to become overly involved emotionally with human reaction to Earth changes that are taking place.

The times that you have been waiting and preparing for are here now. Let those who have ears hear and let those who have eyes see. This activation comes through us as another ray, as another blast of the Creator's presence. The atoms and molecules of your bodies and of your creations are changing, transmuting so rapidly. I ask that you focus the light, that you master your selves concerning your mental and emotional projections, so that you are projecting only that which you desire and only that which is highest wisdom — and surrendering to that which is highest wisdom for you. It is very important for you, for your peace of mind and for your safety and security. It is extremely important for the work that we share in the evolvement of these beings, of the human species on this world.

So meditate. The time for hesitation is over. Love yourselves. Accept yourselves. Nurture yourselves. Heal yourselves. Give yourselves that which you require for your own happiness, joy and security. Come together and share. If you have difficulties meditating alone, gather together and meditate and channel. Support one another at this time. It is very important. Do not hesitate to ask if you are one who needs assistance. Ask us. Ask your loved ones that surround you. Know that great happiness and joy are yours now if you will but indulge in them. I open my heart to you all. I open my heart to all the Starseeds and Light Workers of this world, and to all beings of this world and to the Mother Earth herself. I offer to draw you all into my heart. Some will vote for us and others will not. Be concerned with who you will vote for and not who others are voting for. You are not here to save the "poor mortals." You are here to follow Spirit and in following Spirit you will be doing the most good for all. So until we meet again, on behalf of myself and Ashtar and all of us who love you so much, good night.

↬ THREE ↫

On Meditation

ASHTAR

Good evening. This is Ashtar. It is my pleasure to be with you. I see there are a few hardy souls who have ventured out this evening under the intensified rays of the moon. It will be my endeavor this evening to assist you and to harness some of this intense energy which is present, to assist each of you in opening to more receptivity, more sensitivity to Spirit and guidance. We will simply have to fill the vacant seats with our own people so you do not feel so alone this evening. So we will have a little bit more intimate gathering, which will be pleasant. I would like to speak about meditation this evening, and various related subjects. Above all we will be working to — let me say — escalate your own receptivity and sensitivity to Spirit.

As the energy of this ascension grows within each of you, and within the planet at large, every day can be a new opportunity to go deeper and farther than you have the day before. In fact, it is a continual adjustment on your parts to new guidance and new information, as well as to the ways that you have been practicing your meditations. For everything that you experience is becoming intensified, as the amount of presence, the amount of energy you are feeling grows. You may look out the window at the trees and find that perhaps they may seem more alive today than they did last time you opened to their presence. Perhaps the clouds have a different emanation to you, perhaps they seem more alive. Everything is becoming more alive. The planet itself. All of the beings and all of the manifestations. And you can harness this energy. In fact, it is our intention to help you to harness this energy and put it to maximum use in your lives.

So where to begin? I would say it is good to begin with intention. When you sit to meditate, or when you take a moment in the middle of your day to breathe and focus yourself, what is that which will give you the necessary personal power to blast through the thought patterns and emotional patterns that surround you? It is your intention. Intention is somewhat akin to will power, and yet it is a little bit more simple. It is more a simple statement of purpose, whether it is silent or spoken aloud. Or perhaps it may only be the call of your heart.

There is a moment of recognition within each of you, in your daily lives, and especially prior to your meditations, that you feel a desire to experience Spirit in a deep way, in a meaningful way, in a transforming way — in a way that will assist you with your ultimate goal of ascension. And your intention in doing this is all-important. So I would suggest, as my first meditation tip, to make a practice of stating, either silently or aloud, your intention and your desire. Call upon the masters. Call upon your own higher Selves. Believe me, the manifestation of your own higher Self is not a lesser manifestation than that of Sananda or Ashtar or any of the angelic host. You will learn as you go along that it is very wise to call upon your own higher Self, your own God-self, your own I AM presence. This can be a rather profound experience. Nevertheless, make your desire known. Connect with the desire in your heart, and let it be sincere. So say a bit of a prayer, or an affirmation. This sets the stage. This is like building a foundation or a launching pad. It does more good to sit and state your intention than simply to sit in the meditation position and continue to think about whatever you have been thinking about. It is a way of breaking the patterns, of calling upon the utmost mastery within to assist you in focusing.

I must make this clear. I understand that some of you have been practicing meditation for a long time. You have been working and effectively transforming yourselves, or allowing yourselves to be transformed. Nevertheless, I am here to state that the energy that is manifesting at this time is of more intensity and is of a deeper nature, let us say — and of a more transformative nature — so that your practice and your beliefs and previous experiences of meditation may be in need of expansion. There is an opportunity now to give yourselves entirely to this light — to give yourselves entirely to love, to the presence of your higher Self, and to merge with it. In fact, it is possible now to have a meditation from which you fail to recover! Ultimately your goal, or course, is to manifest the ascension, from which you will not recover. Yet, in the meantime, as you prepare yourselves, know that any meditation you perform, any time you sit or even in the midst of your life, know that you are somewhat playing with fire at this time. Because what you call upon will manifest now.

So I would suggest that you expand your belief systems around meditation. Do not look at it only as something that gives you a little bit of peace, a little help in coping with reality. It is time now to make yourselves a new reality. And it is an excellent opportunity to do so now. For soon the intensity of the emotional release and chaos, apparent chaos, of the world will build to an extent that all of your resources may be required to maintain your focus and to feel the peace, love and light that you may have somewhat taken for granted. Always be appreciative of this experience. Accept it with humility.

So, we are hoping this evening to have a meditation from which none of you recover! By recovering I mean simply returning to your previous patterns of belief and limitation. It is occurring now within all of you that your old patterns and beliefs and understanding, your old ways of existing, are being somewhat shattered, somewhat expanded, and at times this may lead you to feel a little bit up in the air. We have already spoken much about balance, and it is all important at this time. Nevertheless, it is time now to give yourselves entirely to this energy and to meditation, to focusing yourselves. Only by doing this can you ride upon the waves that are manifesting and maintain the balance and the sensitivity to guidance that will assist you in having an enjoyable experience. Many will not be having such an enjoyable experience. You have the opportunity to enjoy yourselves, and in fact, to thrive upon this apparent chaos. For what is chaos to another will to you be felt as extra love and light.

So your intention should be stated, and as you feel yourselves aligning with breath and feeling the presence within you, simply give yourself to that breath. Focus upon it. Allow the energy, the guidance to come and take you where it will. Simply breathe and feel the presence. You may feel an intensity in your mental and emotional bodies, as oftentimes is the case. It is not always easy to meditate to the depths that you desire. I will say that at times like these, affirmations are very powerful — specifically those using the "I AM" prefix.

I will give you an affirmation this evening which is quite powerful, which will assist you in your preparation for ascension. This is one of the I AM affirmations. It is very powerful. "I AM THE RESURRECTION AND THE LIFE." Perhaps you could repeat this silently to yourselves. See how it feels to you.

So if in your practice you find it difficult to concentrate, or you feel yourself drifting, you may use an affirmation such as this: "I AM THE RESURRECTION AND THE LIFE," or "I AM ONE WITH THE LIGHT," — this sort of thing. Saying "I AM" before the affirmation is very powerful. "I AM" is an affirmation of your own higher Self, of your own merging with the light body. Simply to say, "I AM THAT I AM" is an incredibly powerful statement at this time. So use these tools. They are for your pleasure and for your focusing.

And what will you experience? You have all had so much experience. There is a presence within the heart. There is perhaps an intensification of your experience of the Holy Breath. If you focus upon your breath, you will feel the presence that is behind the breath, that is, let me say, driving the breath. It is called the Holy Breath, or the Unspeakable Name of God. It is not speakable because it is not a word. It is a presence, an energy, pre-existent to speech, the very foundation of the universe. It is within you, each of you, connected to your breath. So I would recommend that you not be perhaps so eager to leave your bodies. Sometimes in meditation it is perfectly acceptable to be guided on spiritual adventures, and yet I would say that it is very important at this time to simply be present within your body. Feel your breath and feel the power that is growing within you. The manifestation of the Unspeakable Name. For this is the essence of all that exists, and it is within you as it is within all atoms and all of creation. It is your food. It is that which you can exist and thrive upon. It is that most subtle essence. It is where you come from. That which drives all of your processes. That which energizes your existence and your thoughts and feelings.

So it is time to get to the bottom of all of those manifestations of personality and get to the very Self. What is the Self? This is what must be experienced. It is impossible to describe. Everyone must experience it for themselves. The simplicity of this practice, of simply breathing and focusing is very powerful. You may feel a presence within you that is growing. Perhaps it will feel to you like a channeling, like another being coming down from above into your body. And yet this may simply be your own higher Self. It may be the merging with your light body, the merging with your higher Self. And by practicing this you can, with patience and perseverance, live from the perspective of being merged with the higher Self. This is why we come together in these gatherings and continue to share the experience of what you are. The more often you dip yourself into it, the more it becomes your reality, and your past reality can begin to fade. You need something to replace it with. This is where your higher Self comes in. This is where expansion is required.

So, there is the presence behind the breath. There is also light. You will feel, from time to time, in your meditations, as I am sure many of you have, the magnification of light at your third eye, at your forehead. This is the opening of your spiritual eye, your sixth chakra. And this is how you can see, not with your physical eyes, but with your spiritual eye, your true Self and your divinity. The light that you are is the light of God. So if in your meditations you wish to experience this, it is simply necessary to concentrate and focus your attention upwards a little bit. It is not quite the same as looking upwards with your eyes, but there is a concentration of your inner awareness. And this concentration is generally drawn upwards by the radiation of the light, the inner light.

Upon awakening the third eye center you will receive much more clarity in your guidance. Opening your higher centers allows you to connect more clearly and more profoundly with your guides than you have previously. We have also been discussing channeling a lot lately. Those of you who are experiencing channeling might notice that oftentimes before you channel there is an awakening of your third eye center, an opening. If you focus upon this light within you, upon this internal experience, you will find it easier to receive guidance. It is something like talking and chewing gum at the same time — being conscious of your breathing and viewing the inner light. It takes some practice. But if you can master this you will find your receptivity and your messages growing in power and your channeling will become much more direct.

If you are not desiring channeling, you are probably still wishing to receive messages from your higher Self and from the masters. This is where these practices come in also. Once you are open, you are open to receive. So these practices of meditation will sensitize you to Spirit and desensitize you to pain and suffering. What sensitizes you to Spirit also acts somewhat as an anesthetic to your attachment to limiting emotional experiences and thought patterns.

So what is available to you? This discussion sounds to me rather dry. It does not have the actual experience behind it of what it feels like to be in the state of meditation. Truly, it is a rather juicy experience! There is a lot of love there. There is a great deal of exhilaration. In fact, it could be said that there are no two meditations which are the same. One may look at you and ask why you continue to sit in this way in your life: "Don't you get tired of doing that?" You can answer that you have not been bored yet, because you are experiencing something new and different all the time. The universe is infinite. God's love is infinite. You are infinite. No matter how long you practice this focusing upon Spirit, no matter what states of awareness you achieve, whether you are still in the physical world preparing for ascension or an ascended master, it is the same. You will continue to grow. You will continue to grow using these same simple techniques. Of course, after you have ascended you will have a somewhat different experience. At that point you will be able to manifest a great deal more energy. You will be able to travel, let us say, through the universes within you. At this point it is not possible to give you this intense of an experience. We can only share that which you are capable of. But you are learning to relate more to your higher Selves than to your limited ego selves, and this is an excellent process you are undergoing. It will serve you well.

I will share with you a little bit about my experience of meditation, to help you see why and how this is serving you to go beyond your egos, to identify with your higher Selves. When I sit to meditate, I open to my breath and I call upon my higher Self. Let me say I merge with it instantaneously. It is the same intention that you have, though there is less static, less resistance. My intention alone is of such a magnitude that the very thought of meditation, the very thought of union, puts me in that state. I am sure you have all had the experience at one time or another, where you simply thought about how you would like to be experiencing your higher Self or God and it instantaneously appeared in your consciousness. It is something like that.

How shall I describe this? This is my first attempt at describing my meditation experience to you. Let us say there is a shell, a picture of myself, an energetic structure of my body, while my experience is that behind me and above me I am experiencing universes and galaxies. So I am feeling that my fifth-dimensional expression is maintained, yet the greater portion of my consciousness is expanded to an extent that is very difficult to describe. Let me say that I am aware behind and above me of galaxies swirling. I am aware of consciousness throughout many universes. I am aware of the oneness of all, even while I am maintaining an experience of a limited expression. But at no time am I identifying with the limited expression. It is there as a reference point for me to return to. It is my choice to manifest this expression so that I can do my service, so that I can do the work that I have given myself to. My experience of meditation feeds me and serves me in the same way that yours does you. And it is my intention to assist you all, as it is the intention of all of the masters, to take you as far as you can go, to the highest manifestation of meditation you can experience from within your physical form — or let me say — from within the *illusion* of being within the physical form.

So you will be finding your lives transforming. You will be finding yourselves feeling a bit more that life is dreamlike, and that it is necessary for you to have a continual experience, or at least a very regular experience, of your unlimited Self as a frame of reference. So just as I use my meditation practice as a frame of reference — as my spiritual food and sustenance and pleasure and exhilaration and joy — so will you. So you do now, and so will you to an even greater extent. It is time to go beyond. Whether you are just now beginning meditation practice, or whether you are an old hand at it, the call to you is the same. It is time to go beyond. There is no limit to what you can experience within yourselves.

And there is no higher perspective you can achieve than to be inside and within yourself. You are, from time to time, drawn to the tutelage of various masters. Sometimes you may be aware that you are being lifted and taken to another etheric realm, perhaps to the ships. Perhaps to another world. Perhaps to one of your master's drawing rooms. These experiences will be continuing with you as you give yourself to the process. Yet these occur only as instruction for you, only for specific purposes. The goal of your awakening is to connect with your own divinity, your own Self, which is the Self of God.

So I am telling you that you can experience incredible depths of light and presence. You can experience oneness with God. You can experience enlightenment, the merging of yourself with your higher Self, or God. All of this can be experienced by you prior to your ascension. It has been experienced by many beings.

So my dear ones, it is time for you to learn of your own magnificence, of your own power and of your own ability to go beyond into higher realms of experience and greater depths of love. We have been working with your receptivity, with the opening of your higher centers and your heart center. We are enhancing your ability to perceive, opening your channels. We are opening the receptors within your brains and your higher chakras, to strengthen your connection.

It is difficult for me at this moment to speak. I am feeling such love. But I offer myself to you for any questions you have. Let me say that I put myself at your disposal this evening, out of love. And I am experiencing so much love for each of you. It is as if I am being allowed to experience the love of the Creator for each of you, which is profound. From this vantage point I offer myself. If you have questions concerning meditation, if you have questions of any sort, please consider this a time for us to share together. I am here to benefit you in any way I can. If you desire, you may simply continue your meditation. Know that it is a blessed evening and you are receiving blessings. We have succeeded in our attempt to harness this energy and focus it. So what questions might you have this evening?

"I have a question. Why are spiritual seekers attracted to Mt. Shasta? And if you could, say something about that place and about the energy that is there and what is going on there that attracts us."

Well, let me say that Mt. Shasta is a place where the purity of the Creator's manifestation is quite profound. There is an etheric presence there of Spirit which is cleansing to the atmosphere surrounding the mountain and cleansing to all who enter the aura of the mountain. It is a place of magnification of the higher Self. Because of this purity, it is a retreat of the ascended masters also. There are, within the mountain, beneath the mountain, chambers and halls created by the ascended masters. Here they can gather and have meetings and meditations and take counsel and comfort in one another's presence. It is a focal point of ascended master activity. There are many wonders there, and perhaps one day, if you are fortunate you will be allowed to enter. A few beings have been, prior to their ascension, allowed to enter and have spoken of what they have experienced. But know that regardless of whether or not you are guided into the internal areas of the mountain, you do receive a great deal of purification and blessing. You might also say that the higher you go on the mountain, the more powerful the manifestation, the more pure the energy. That is, the vortex point of this particular mountain is most pronounced from the upper half upwards. So if you can get to an elevation of 7000 feet or higher, the energy is more powerful. Nevertheless, the entire area is blessed.

So for you I think it is a place to go and to leave behind your cares, a place to transcend and to open a new chapter in your life perhaps — a new chapter in your spiritual growth — by rising to an elevation that is somewhat above much of the emotional chaos that is prevalent in the world, to gain guidance and direction. I would say for you in particular, let it be a place to go to retreat and to receive guidance and direction concerning the next phase of your life. Be open and have an open slate, let us say, upon which the masters can write their greetings and their guidance to you, give you the options that are available to you based upon your level of evolvement and your attainments.

"Ashtar, I am praying to have an experience in the ascension chair that Godfrey Ray King had an experience in. I was just wondering, is that something that is available to us before we ascend or is that part of the process? Could you talk about that?"

So you want to sit in the electric chair! This is a technology which is available and which will be utilized upon your ascension. It is part of the process. It may not be in the form of a chair, but you will be subjected to high voltage. High voltage etheric and spiritual energy which will complete your ascension process. So your longing is something which will be gratified. So, this brings up an interesting area. I will not go into it too deeply, but there is an aspect of ascension which is somewhat technological in nature. And when you are lifted into the ships, or if you are fortunate enough to be one who is able to manifest ascension prior to this, you can experience this. The ascension chair is something which has been used by the ascended masters to assist those who are at a certain state of readiness, those who are at a certain state of preparation, to complete their ascension in a quite dramatic way. It is somewhat of a labor saving device. So many of you who attain to the lifting into the ships and to the ascension will experience this.

We have much high technology at our disposal. And of course the ascended masters in their earthly retreats have access and utilize these same technologies. I will say to you that it will not be long before you are ascended, though it may seem long if you are anxiously awaiting. It is a time for all of you to be patient and mature in your growth and in your outlook. I have said before that it is for you to be prepared to go at any time, and yet be willing to stay and be a servant, a servant for as long as is required. It will not be long. I do not see it being long before you have this experience. In fact, the longing that you have within you is an aspect that is important. It is a necessary factor in your growth and in your attaining to ascension. You must have the experience of that feeling of devotion and longing within you. This is why we have spoken of it so much — to tempt you, let me say — to share with you the benefits and the experience a little bit so that you will have this longing. And this longing is what will ultimately help you to go through the final choice and selection. The final moment of your choice. This longing creates the inertia to do this, so it is part of the process.

Sometimes one feels such a longing to be with God, to be merged with God, that tears of devotion will arise. This is a blessed state, though you may feel yourself somewhat in emotional pain. It is a sense of longing. A sense of unfulfillment and a knowledge that fulfillment is at hand, or can be at hand. A longing to be with the Divine. A longing to be One. So this a different form of suffering than the suffering that you may have been used to. It is a blessed form of suffering. I would not even call it suffering. I would call it a blessed emotion. It has a purpose. It unlocks the heart and opens you to greater depth of experience.

"Ashtar, how is our critical mass doing?"

I would say the critical mass in this room is quite profound. It can be difficult for those of you who are preparing for the ascension. I can see that it is difficult at times to be patient. I would suggest you channel your energies into communication and sharing this process with others. There is a definite intensification which has taken place even within the last months. I am not party to the actual amount of energy, let us call it, required to trigger the ascension. This is known by the Father. So I am with you in waiting patiently, and I am ready. In fact we have the hall decorated and are waiting for you. Fortunately, our decorations do not deteriorate, so they will be as fresh as ever when they are fully utilized!

You must be primarily focused upon the critical mass within yourself. And of course the critical mass, or the energy that is upon the planet is intensifying. In fact at this full moon it is intensifying a great deal. I would recommend that you all focus yourselves during and immediately after the days of the full moon. It may be that the final lifting will occur at such a time. It seems probable to me. I am speculating, as you may speculate. You must understand that being ascended does not grant you the experience of being all-knowing. So I have my limitations as you do. It is for me to await my orders and to assist you in whatever way I can. We are putting our feelers out a great deal to attract more volunteers for ascension. There is a great excitement within this town, for example, for ascension, and within the second ascension class. There are many eager volunteers — even after one class, I think they are quite excited by the prospects. I would say that each of you can assist by sharing this information with those who are open to receive it.

So you have a responsibility here to yourselves, and if you accept it, a responsibility to assist this process in creating the critical mass. It may seem like a big job, but perhaps if each one of you were to attract only one more person to the ascension process, it would be sufficient. I am observing the energy growing. I am observing the intensification of the light upon the Earth plane. It is growing daily. Things are going rather well, but there can be a great deal more done. There are many areas of the Earth which are suffering quite heavily. And there are many lights that are visible to us upon the surface. Especially in California, especially in the United States, and in selected other areas. But the overall plan is going along as projected.

"In the lifting process is it easier to lift people from certain areas than others?"

It is easier to lift anyone who is prepared, regardless of their location. So you need not be overly concerned about where you are. It is more to be concerned where you are in your consciousness. Those of you who are aware of this process will understand in those last few hours that it is time to be attentive to your inner self. The intensity will grow, and as you have experienced a little bit this evening, when the intensity is very profound it is natural to go within and to give yourself to it. So you do not have to fear missing the boat if you are preparing. We have quite an extensive communications network wherein we monitor each of you day to day, and especially those of you who are giving yourselves to the ascension process. You are known to us. We have moment to moment consciousness of your experience. In fact we are listening in on everything you say and feel. I promise I will not hold it against you! There is no judgment on our part. It is our way of keeping a connection with you, so that when the time occurs, since we do not know when it will occur, we have you in our sights. All of the Starseeds on this planet are known to us, especially those who have been preparing.

So again, this evening I have been speaking about meditation and how you can connect with your higher Self, your true power. And know, whether you are totally conscious of it or not, you are gods and goddesses. You are ascended beings under cover. You are creating your own resistance movement here. You have parachuted into this strange environment. You are surrounded by foreign powers. You do not necessarily have an easy time speaking their language. But you have received sufficient training in previous incarnations so that you can speak the same language. Because this is the language you will be using to communicate these blessed events. Know that you are expanded beings. And I am sure you are beginning to be more aware of this. One being coming into alignment with this ascension process affects the entire process. It affects the entire critical mass. One being. One meditation on your parts affects the critical mass. So do not feel helpless. Empower yourselves.

So if there are no more questions, perhaps we could just do a little more meditation. It is not my desire to have you all explode this evening, but I think you can handle a little bit more. And I would like to request that you experiment with the affirmation we have given previously. The affirmation is quite effective in assisting your meditations, and specifically, in drawing forth the magnification of your higher Self and your light body. That is, "I AM THE RESURRECTION AND THE LIFE." So speak this softly to yourselves and then we will breathe together and meditate a bit.

Well, again, let me thank you for your attention this evening. I am aware that we have discussed meditation many times before, but I felt it important to tell you what I told you once again — and to work with you at this critical time, on this important evening, to open you a little bit farther. And we have done so successfully. Know that your connection with me and with the other masters is growing stronger each day, as many of you can attest. Your ability to receive guidance and messages is growing, and your awareness of who you are and your ability to trust in Spirit. You will be called upon to trust more and more, and you will be able to trust more because you will have an intensified connection. So the work that we are doing energetically is extremely important. We love you and look forward to seeing you again. Good night.

∽ Four ∽

The Harvest

Sananda

Good evening. Nice to be here with you. This is Sananda. So how are you all adjusting to the autumn? Getting darker, getting cooler in the evenings. You are adapting, are you not? The autumn is inevitable to you. It is something that you know must come. Though you may long for the longer days and the warmer weather, it is inevitable. You have experienced it before. You know there is nothing you can do but enjoy it, for the beauty that it brings, for the necessity that it is in the overall cycle of life.

There are other cycles. Larger cycles. More impressive, I would say, that you are also experiencing. You are at the end of a grand cycle. And just as you must adapt and acquiesce to the inevitability of the autumn, so must you adapt and surrender to the grand cycle that is occurring now. You all are aware that though you may long for the sunshine, and you may in fact do whatever you can to resist the autumn's falling, it is inevitable. And so it is with this grand cycle that is now coming to a close.

You could say that it is harvest time on many levels. And just as it does you little good to resist the autumn's falling, so it is the same with the grand cycle that you are within. It is for you to adapt, to surrender to the process, to the harvest time that you are experiencing. It is a time that tends to bring out uncertainties within your emotional makeup and in your mental bodies, as it is not something that has occurred with the inevitable regularity of the annual autumn. It is something that occurs once in many thousands of years.

So, this transformation is not something that you have grown accustomed to. You pretty much know what to expect from the autumn. You know that it will go into the winter, and so the winter will go into the spring, and you will get your sunshine back again. With the grand cycle, things are not quite so apparent to you. So we are here to reassure you, to try to assist you in adapting to the changes that are occurring, these changes in the very structure of reality as you have known it. It is our hope that these changes will not take you by surprise, but that you will be well prepared for them — in fact, looking forward to them. I think most of you are. In fact, I think most of you are ready for something. The limitation and the suffering of the Earth plane need to come to an end, and come to an end they will.

So, whereas in your autumn season the sunlight diminishes, in the harvest season I am speaking of, the light grows stronger. It is the light of the Creator, returning to take you home again, returning to realign you and reconnect you within the heavenly circuits of the universal creation. You could say that the Earth has been existing a little bit out of the loop of the universe, out of the loop of ordinary creative evolution. And now it is being reconnected again. The systems are being reconnected, and all things will return to a more normal evolutionary status.

In order for this to occur, as you know, there will be some housecleaning that is necessary. This is being taken care of. I am sure you are all feeling a little bit swept out inside lately. It is part of the process. You are a microcosm of your planetary sphere. The planetary sphere is a macrocosm of you as a collective of individuals. So the power is being turned on again. And it is flowing through the circuits into this portion of this local universe, affecting every one of you and every one on this planet and the planet as a whole. It is coming as a boost, a boost to your energetic fields, a boost to your spiritual essences.

In the past you may have wandered through this life, through this world, feeling you were on a starvation diet of truth, a starvation diet of love and light. Receiving a little bit to keep you going, but never enough to fully satisfy. It was something that seemed to be in short supply here. In fact, it was in short supply. No longer will this be the case. I think now you will have to adapt yourselves to receiving a great deal of spiritual nutrition in the form of light energy.

There is an experience that you may be aware of in your scientific studies of evolution. It is called adaptation. Every species over the course of time adapts to its surroundings. This is a natural law. One aspect of this adaptation is that if the external circumstances change too radically, it makes it much more difficult for species to adapt to the changes, and some species will become obsolete, will become extinct. And so it is at this time. The changes are occurring very quickly. You may feel that you have been waiting for them for a long time, but in truth, the change is occurring very quickly.

The challenge to the human species is to adapt to this changing environment, to adapt to this new diet of intensified spiritual presence and light. You could say that this is causing a bit of stress on the species as a whole, as certain members are adapting more readily than others. And I say to you it is most likely that many individuals of the species will not adapt to this, will not adapt to this ascension that is occurring on a planetary scale. Only those who are open and surrendered and adaptable will be able to experience consciously the full benefit of this change, and will learn to enjoy it more and more as it progresses. So consider yourselves quite fortunate to be among those who are aware of this transformation — you who have the ways and means within yourselves, who have the support internally and externally to assist in this transformation and to be able to adapt to it.

It is a natural law. It is quite scientific in one way. You could say the energy or the vibration of the planet is changing from a third-dimensional frequency band — more solid, more dense — to that of the fifth-dimension, which is much higher in frequency. As you know, this causes the release processes you have been experiencing, and will continue to experience for some time. This is adaptability. Your release work is another way of adapting, of letting go of the dense energies so you can hold within your bodies more of the light.

So I am encouraging all of you to increase your awareness of what is occurring on a global scale, and also on a spiritual scale within yourselves. It is no longer appropriate to hold your heads in the sand and think that everything will be as it always was, that what you used to rely on for your reality frame of reference will always be there. It will not always be there. It is time to adapt.

And within this cycle, within this transformation that is occurring, there are various levels. There are various waves of energy that are coming through. You could say that the energy is increasing in waves, more than as a constant. There is generally an overall increase in the frequency of energy that is coming through now to you, but it comes in waves. There is a wave, and then there is a trough or plateau. A time of integration, a time of balancing and adapting to that level or frequency of energy. For example, the past two months or so have been to you a period of less intense energy and more a time of integration.

We are in another wave at this time. I am sure many of you are experiencing this. A re-intensification of your processing and of your spiritual experiences. The energy that is coming through now, and which will come through for the next two months at least, will be again a much stronger and more powerful emanation. It will again require you to adapt, to receive, to open to more miracles in your lives, to more love and light and joy, as well as to more adaptability.

If you will look at the reality you existed in, even a very short time ago in your lives, I think you will notice that you are in a new reality. You are experiencing things from a different perspective, from a higher understanding and a higher awareness. And so it will continue. So that in two months time, you will look back at this period and say, "Well, I have grown an incredible amount in these two months." In fact you will have. In fact the planet will have. There is no more time to wait. There is no more reason to wait for the ascension to occur. It is occurring. It is as inevitable as the autumn. It is inevitable, the harvest of beings.

Just as the grain in the field must be harvested at the perfect moment, the most opportune moment to insure the maximum yield and the maximum ripeness, so it is with the planet Earth. The beings of the Earth are the grains, and regardless of whether or not all of them are ripe, it is time for the ones that are ripe to be harvested and taken into that higher dimension of experience. If this did not occur it would be a long wait for another cycle to come around. This is not possible. The Creator has a master plan, and you here in your experience of this Earth and of your blossoming divinity are a part of that plan.

The Creator has bestowed His presence within each of you, so that you can have a personal relationship with Him. You can have a personal relationship with that Creator through your I AM presence, and with the assistance of His many messengers, His hierarchy of spiritual teachers. And indeed it is time for you to take your rightful place in the universe. You individually as Starseeds, and also this planet collectively. It is time. It is time to return, it is time to re-integrate within the circuits of cosmic evolution. It is time to do away with this thing you have come to know as death. And these pains and sorrows that you have accepted as part of life which are truly not intended to be.

You see, you have adapted to your situations. You have made the best of it. Well, there is another reality that is to be adapted to which is much more pleasant. It does not involve death. It is endless growth and endless beauty and love. It is an unfolding. It is perfection perfecting itself. And it is time for this planet to be re-integrated into that program. And time for those beings who have not the capacity to integrate and to adapt to be taken elsewhere to other planets that have time. The Earth has no more time for this. This is not a judgment or a criticism of any beings. This is merely a statement of the fact that the cycle is complete and that it is time.

Many times you who are of the light, you who are the Starseeds have asked, "What of those beings who are not prepared for the New Age? What will happen to them?" And you might view them as "those poor souls." Well I say to you, those poor souls would be just as happy to be rid of you as you might be to have them evolve. So, you see, the restructuring that is going to take place will be to the benefit of all and will be to the enjoyment of all. Those beings who long to create wars and strife and live to be warrior spirits will go on to planets where they can remain warriors, and that will be their way of life. And they will be most happy there.

You yourselves would consider it a hell. They themselves might consider it a heavenly activity.

So you see there is no place for your judgment and criticism here. It is for you to accept the higher wisdom. The wisdom that is truly beyond human understanding. In fact there are no beings I know of who have true and full access to the wisdom of the Creator, who have full understanding of His mind, of His full intentions and vision. We are operating on what we have to go on, based upon our previous experience and the direction and guidance we have received, just as you are. We have a bit more experience of that divinity, as our veils have been removed. Your veils are also being removed. And yet the master plan is so all encompassing, is so impossible to fathom. Infinite love in action is the best way I can describe it at this time. And this you too will see, as you re-enter the evolutionary spiral at a more advanced stage. You will, I think, also come to appreciate the incredible wisdom and the incredible love that has gone into this divine plan for the creations. For there is no end to the joy and light and love you can experience. And this expansion of consciousness, this expansion of the presence of joy and bliss, the feeling of the Creator, just grows and grows. And you can continue on that evolutionary spiral, through the hierarchy of the grand universe, ever spiraling on your way.

You know, when you were a child and perhaps you had your friends over, you know how intent you were in your play. You could say you were focusing one hundred percent of your attention and your enthusiasm into that play. You were making the most of those moments. And as a child does, when it was time to be called home at the end of the day, many times you would rebel and say, "No, I want to continue to play longer. Please don't make me go home. I want to stay and play with my friends. We are having fun."

Well, you are all going to have your opportunity for this endless play. You have begun already, and it just grows and grows. You don't get tired or sleepy or cranky. You don't have to stop and eat unless you want to. You never have to leave the companions that you love to be with. And you never have to do homework! In fact you could say your play is a course of study in itself, and your play becomes your work, your service, and you become fully integrated in such a way that the longing of your heart is identical to that which you are engaged with in your service activities. There is a perfect place and perfect opportunities for every one of you. So if you have felt out of place here in this world, trying to fit in, it is because it is not a place that you can fit in to. It is a place that you are here to experience and to learn from and to teach for a short time, and then to move on. This is as close to homework that you are going to get — your Earth lives.

So, as I have said, things are going to be stepping up a little bit again. Most of you have had experience of this in the past, the intensification of the light and its ramifications to you. I trust you will all be very chameleon-like in your adaptability. You are learning to become more streamlined in your approach to life and in your conscious awareness. You have learned how to release densities, how to accept more light and love.

So you have situated yourselves, you have positioned yourselves very well for this next phase. I congratulate you on your wisdom, on your openness. I encourage you in the days and weeks and months ahead to give yourself more to your spiritual practices, knowing that you will receive much more than you put into it by way of your own efforts. And make yourselves available to your spiritual guidance, for there will be much of guidance coming through to you. And you will require this assistance in order to have a graceful and smooth and enjoyable adaptation to the light. You see, those who resist the light will have a different experience from those who are surrendered and open and welcoming it.

Most in the world, most on this planetary sphere, are in a position of resisting growth. There are very few who are welcoming it. And there is a great need for those who can do this and can share this experience with others. You are those. You are the group, you are members of the group that exists throughout the globe at this time, the Light Workers. And because you are more sensitive, you are experiencing these energies and these changes a bit ahead of others who are not quite so sensitive. This will benefit you in the long run. You are coming into the clear, so to speak. Your changes will not be nearly so intense as those who have not prepared themselves.

So I encourage you to continue to give yourself to your spiritual practice. Follow your guidance. Trust in your guidance. Know that just as the light is intensifying, so will your guidance and so will your support be intensifying. You are learning to dine on this light. You are learning to live on that. You are learning to be dependent upon that light, upon that Creator, rather than upon limited realities that are ever crumbling around you. So this is your sanctuary. This is your joy, your love and peace. It is within you.

You are going to be experiencing much transformation in the days ahead. Those of you who are open to your channeling abilities, to your contact with us of the higher dimensions, will experience more powerful visitations if you are inclined to welcome us. You will be experiencing the relinquishing of many of your limiting self-concepts. You will come into a greater appreciation of yourselves for who you are, not for who you think you need to be. More self love will be coming your way, and in fact, self love is critical to the adaptation process. You will witness in the world around you much chaos and confusion. I am sure you are already seeing it everywhere you turn. You may witness an increase in Earth changes, this sort of thing. So the shakeup is beginning to occur. It will intensify, as you know. And it will be to you as validation for your experience, as validation for the truth that you have discovered within yourselves.

Always know that we are with you. You are never alone. You may feel yourselves alone at times, but if you do it is because you are in need of that experience in order to release or process. Your Earth school experiences will push your buttons as required and only as required. But there is more processing that you need to go through. A little bit more, I would say.

Each of you are unique; your own paths are unique. You are like many beautiful spiraling vines growing up, each in your own unique way towards the sun. Your goal is the same. Your paths are different. So honor your own paths and know that you are growing just as you are supposed to grow. And if you will apply your-selves to your spiritual practice you will know this to be a fact, rather than a belief that is only intellectual. You will know it as a fact. And you will be able to sur-render and trust that which is alive within you. And you will be able to adapt to these changes. In fact, I think that they will be enjoyable to you.

The difference here between enjoying these changes and not is a resistance factor. Giving yourself to your meditation and spiritual practices releases you from that resistance and frees you to the enjoyment of the process. And there is a definite need for those who know how to enjoy this process, who know how to surf on these waves. There is no end of people who are struggling and swimming and bobbing up and down in the water trying to keep their heads afloat, struggling just to get enough air. There is a definite need for more beings who are surfing, who are high and dry and enjoying the ride. This is your role at this time. It is important. It is your responsibility.

If you accept your responsibility as teachers, it will make it easier for you to do that which is required to maintain your high and dry state and your enjoyment. So accept your destinies. Accept your guidance. Accept your paths with responsibility. Know that you have chosen them. Know that the beings that you are will be unfolded. Your divinity is to be made clear more and more. It is going to be less and less possible for you to hide within your limited self concepts. You will be shaken loose of those — gently, it is my hope. It is a gradual, beautiful unfoldment — an inevitable unfoldment to be enjoyed, and to be adapted to in those times when you feel challenged.

The times that are upon you now are going to be profound, yet quickly passing. And the changes that you experience will not be long. You will process much in a very short time. And you will be very grateful for the opportunities and for the results of this. So understand this. What is occurring now, in these years, is but the twinkling of one star, one infinitesimal moment in time. So try not to be too wrapped up in your dramas. These are very small in the great scheme of things. Very small. If you give yourself to your spiritual practice you will understand and experience them through a higher perspective. If you indulge in your dramas they will become all encompassing. Perhaps you will forget you are walking around on a planet at all. You will think you are in some other reality. You will forget everything. It is time for remembering, not for forgetting. So don't forget to breathe!

So my friends, have you any questions for me this evening? I know you are all digesting my words.

"As we begin to accept our roles of being teachers and learning to see ourselves outside of our self-imposed limits, many of our fellow beings on the planet will not choose the ascension for one reason or another. Are we then to teach those who might be called light sleepers, those who are still awakening?"

Yes, you are to be here for them as they awaken. They may not be awakened so much by your particular words and actions as much as by the increased energy and the Earth change activities, this sort of thing. There is much that is occurring to awaken beings at this time. Every effort is being given to this. It is more that you are those who are acting somewhat as a safety net to catch those who fall out of sleep.

"A little support, then."

Yes. You are those who they can look at and say, "I don't have to do it this way. I don't have to suffer. I can be happy and understand what is occurring to me in my life." And you are those who will be as examples, it is my hope. So your service in this is to teach and to share where those beings are open. You will serve as examples, as ones who have something to share. They will find you, the ones that need to find you. And you will find your right places and your right ways of serving. Service becomes more and more a matter of simply being yourself and doing what comes naturally to you.

Sometimes I am aware that those beings that we discuss this with can tend to become fearful, thinking that, "Oh my goodness! Now I am going to have to be a world teacher." And they envision all sorts of activities that they are scared to death to perform. Well, I assure you that all great world teachers are simply engaged in the act of being themselves. And they are simply growing in their responsibility and in their awareness, uncovering that longing that is within them to serve. They are in alignment with their true destinies and to them it is quite natural. It is not without challenges, but it is easier to go along with your divine destiny than to avoid it. So allow that to unfold for you and you will be in for very pleasant surprises. This goes for all of you — all of you world teachers surrounding me this evening.

"I have a question, Sananda. This wave of energy that is coming in now. How long will it last, and is it a wave that some of us will be ascending on?"

I would say two to three months of intense activity is scheduled. It will vary according to your own process, you see. Those who have more density to release will experience more processing. Those who have released much, who are positioning themselves in their consciousness to be themselves and to awaken naturally and gradually will experience less. With regards to the ascension, it is always a possibility.

"I am getting the feeling that part of our training is having experiences that we are afraid to experience. Is that true? Sort of like going through fears that you don't really want to experience so that you are able to release fears. Is that true?"

Yes. You are all on a path of unfoldment, and it is oftentimes frightening to you at various times, having

to go beyond your limited security, your limited awareness of yourself. Every time you go through this —
another step in your unfoldment — there is a tendency
for fear to creep in and to tell you, "No, don't go
through this door. It will be too intense for you. You
don't know what's on the other side. You are not up to
the task." All of those fears and doubts are the result of
limited self-concepts you have adopted through your
Earth experience. The world is very good at teaching
you that you are less, that you are small and powerless
beings, dependent upon governments and churches
and dollars — this sort of thing. You are dependent
only upon the Creator.

So I think it is time for us to meditate together a
little bit. I would like to speak longer, but this is not
my body! So we will have just a brief meditation this
evening.

Relax yourselves. Pull your concentration and your
attentiveness into your bodies, into your breath. Bring
your breath down all the way into your bellies. Allow
your bodies to relax. Release your thoughts and your
cares and your reactions to my discourse. Let your
hearts open a little bit. And we will bring through some
healing energy for you, to assist you in your adaptability.

So my dear friends, thank you for your time and energy this evening. Thank you for your attentiveness in meditation. You may continue if you desire, but it is time for me to depart from this body. I will be with you, if you desire, for some time to come, if you would like to meditate longer. Love yourselves. Be in joy and peace. Don't forget to breathe. Until next time, good night.

✑ FIVE ✑

Self-Mastery and Manifestation

ST. GERMAIN

Hello. This is St. Germain. Get comfortable. I am going to be speaking about self-mastery and manifestation, and the interrelatedness of these two areas. Afterwards we may have a bit of a bonfire. So I hope you brought your marshmallows. If not, you will have to manifest some. That's a good place to start — manifesting marshmallows. It's much easier than manifesting automobiles and dollars. It's good to start out small and work your way up. It gives you confidence in the process. We will also be doing some gardening this evening.

So — self-mastery. How do you get to be an ascended master? By the path of self-mastery. To be a master you must have mastered yourself, your own manifestations, your own being, your own thoughts and emotions. You must have purified yourself, or allowed yourself to be purified by giving yourself to the light. The path of spiritual growth and self-mastery is somewhat akin to gardening. Your life is like a garden. You wander through your gardens, and there you see before you all of your creations, all the manifestations of what you have thought, felt and believed in your lifetime. And it is for you to be the caretakers of your gardens. It is for you to be responsible for what is growing there. It is for you to be the gardener of your experience, and to assume responsibility for the care and maintenance of your own earthly experience — all that you have within you, all that is yours.

Upon assuming responsibility for these thoughts, feelings, emotions, and manifestations, at all levels of yourself, it is time for you to do your gardening work. Perhaps some weeding is in order. It is for you to learn to nurture those plants which you desire, which are beautiful and serving you, and to prune away some of the dead and useless underbrush. Perhaps you need to pull some weeds. You have all been doing this in your lives. In fact, it is rather difficult to avoid this process, there is so much energy and light flowing through your bodies and your beings. It is becoming more and more difficult to look the other way and ignore what is growing within you. Your attention is being called continuously to what is within yourself, and to the reflections that you receive of yourself from your external experiences. They are all reflections of what is growing within your own garden, all reflections of the current state of affairs in your own emotional and mental bodies. So whatever you are reaping externally is what you have growing within you. You have fed certain parts of yourselves. Those are the parts which you have given nurturance to and which will be strong. There are other parts which you have not given your full attention to, and they may need some additional care in order for you to become balanced.

So, in a way you could say that self-mastery is mastering your own feelings and thoughts. It is paying attention to what you are creating, to the seeds you are sowing in each moment. It is in the past that the seeds were sown for this moment of experience. So self-mastery is attending to what you are creating in this moment, so that you may experience what you desire to experience in future moments. You want to plant only the seeds that you desire to bring forth in your life. This requires attentiveness to your creations, to what you are feeding with your attention. How does this garden grow? How do you plant these seeds? By your attention. There is no water required in this garden. It is the water of your own attention. Whatever you give your attention to, that is what you will be nurturing and feeding and what will be growing in your lives. So if you desire to reap positive rewards and experiences you must sow positive seeds. You will never create a perfect and refined atmosphere within your own natures by sowing seeds of hatred or anger, by continuing to create these experiences.

There is an incredible amount of grace that is flowing. There is an incredible amount of support for your growth experiences. Yet free will still has the absolute final word in what you create in your lives. So if you are attempting to plant seeds of spiritual growth and happiness, the ascended masters will assist you in every way to nurture these creations. And yet there is nothing we can do if you feed, nurture, and continue to give your attention to other areas. This is your free will. This is how you learn. The Earth garden is where you learn. It has become quite overgrown, as you know. And the cure for the garden Earth is to begin with the garden within yourselves, to perfect that and make it beautiful and radiant. Then you can be an example to others. Then you can sow seeds of beauty and love and light.

I must make a distinction here. There is much occurring in the area of processing your emotions, your past karma. And it does no good to deny this experience. We are not saying you should deny your experiences or your emotions. What we are discussing are your creations, that which you are creating in this moment and in the future. It is still necessary for you to process and deal with all you have created in the past, by your beliefs and impressions and thoughts. It is for you to do some weeding and pruning, and this is where the processing comes in. As you attain to a level of mastery, you will reach a point where you no longer create any negativity. You will only create that which is positive. And at that point you can deal finally with the remnants and residue of your past creations, anything that is remaining within you that is not positive. You see, you can remove, in a very gentle and loving way, all that is imperfect within yourselves. It sounds like a big job sometimes. I do not mean to give you that impression. What I am saying is that if you create positivity in your life, your life will be so much easier. You will have less resistance to the energy that is flowing through at this time, the energy of spiritual growth, the energy of the ascended masters, the extraterrestrial brotherhood that are here to guide and assist you on your path of ascension. If you wish to achieve maximum growth, it is for you to assume responsibility and self-mastery. There are no ascended masters who have not attained self-mastery. That is why they are called masters.

So, what I am suggesting to you this evening is simply that you be attentive to what you are creating, to your reactions to life. Life is your teacher. It will give you reflections of what you have believed, reflections of what you have created by your thoughts and attention. There is a certain point where you must draw the line, where you must cut the cords and bonds of inertia. There is an inertia in all types of activity. You have an inertia towards meditation if you meditate regularly. You have an inertia towards love if you love regularly. You have an inertia towards abundance if you are abundant. You also have inertia towards things you have accepted in the past, in your beliefs and feeling natures, that are less positive. If you are a person who tends to become angry when you are stressed, you have an inertia within you towards this response. So there comes a certain point where through your attentiveness, you realize this — that you are, by your own attention, feeding this inertia. And perhaps this inertia is limiting your experience of the higher Self and the road that you wish to take. There is a point where you must somehow turn your back upon your inertia and simply let it lie there. You must discontinue feeding that particular response.

There is so much grace, so many blessings flowing now. When you sit and meditate you will find this is true. Yet still there is no way you can simply meditate away all your weeds. There is some gardening which has to be done and some processing. And all of this processing is taking you to a state of purity. This does not mean that you will not have earthly desires. As long as you are on the Earth you will have earthly desires. So we are not teaching a monastic experience. We are teaching responsibility and integrity within your response to those desires. It's a different thing. It is more subtle and refined. This is the Age of Aquarius now. This is not the Piscean Age. In that age you could go live in a monastery and feel that you had things taken care of. It's more demanding now, but the rewards are much greater. Very few people ascended during the Piscean Age. There will be a mass ascension in this age. This path is leading you towards the ascension. This is the most important benefit of tending your gardens and taking responsibility for your manifestations. In the meantime, another fringe benefit is that you will learn and understand the laws of manifestation. By attending to your creations, that which you have already created in your life, and that which you will create, you will gain knowledge of how manifestation works. You will learn how to create all that is in alignment with your highest good — the abundance that you desire, the love that you require, the comforts, the spiritual experiences, the gifts of the Spirit that you desire. It is all part of the same process. With self-mastery, you can manifest directly and easily. Without self-mastery, you are sabotaging your attempts to manifest by continuing old inertia that has sabotaged you in the past. It is time for you who are on this path to assume this responsibility in your lives. This is not a path that can be accomplished overnight. It may take some patience and perseverance on your part. When you first sit down to meditate it can be difficult to focus your mind deeply enough to truly manifest the experience of meditation. If you apply yourself to this, you will find that you get better and better at it. It becomes easier and easier. And after some time you find that you can meditate at any moment that you desire. You can connect with your higher Self, with your mighty I AM presence, with your guidance. It is very simple because you have applied yourself and manifested some perseverance in attaining your goal. So it is the same with manifestation. If you have a great deal of inertia that sabotages your attempts to manifest prosperity, let us say, you can sit and say many affirmations for prosperity, and perhaps you will only find that you are processing old beliefs. And so you do not manifest that new automobile instantaneously. It requires a little bit of self-mastery, of weeding and persistence. I am here to tell you that it is within your grasp. All the universe is opening its doors to you to make every ounce of your effort worth pounds and pounds of results.

So perhaps in the past you attempted to do affirmations or meditations or certain techniques to help you manifest, and grew frustrated with them. I suggest you try again. Try some experiments in your lives. Try to manifest a bag of marshmallows. Then work on that automobile. Start in small ways. Affirm for what you desire. And take responsibility for the process of caring for your garden and turning your back on your old inertia. Perhaps you are a person who gets angry. You have that moment of choice in your experience. You have the split second of conscious choice between the time that someone riles you up and the time that you react. If you will pay attention, you will notice there is a split second there, in which you decided how to react. This is your window of escape from inertia. In that moment of decision, make the decision not to respond with anger. Make the decision to respond with patience and love. And this applies to any reaction or emotion. You will find that as you attempt mastery you will come face to face with these inertias and experiences.

So, in making the attempt to go within and to manifest that which you desire, the first thing that you will encounter is this garden. You will see the condition of the garden and will recognize those areas that need more work. And there you will find your path to mani-festation. Sometimes the most direct path to the manifestation of a goal will take you through a lot of emotional processing. You may be dealing with some issues with your parents, or your past, or some other aspect which seemingly has no relationship to that manifestation. And yet you are dealing with those things which have sabotaged you in the past, with those feelings and beliefs which have limited you and perhaps made you feel that you deserved less. You did not deserve less. Each of you in this room deserve abundance, love and prosperity of all kinds. You deserve to manifest what you desire instantaneously. It is for you simply to finish cleaning up your gardens a little bit more. Continue on your paths, and meditate, so you will have the awareness of what it is you need work on. Meditation will lead you directly to guidance, or intuitive feelings, and you will find yourself treading easily through the underbrush.

So whatever you need you can have. I suggest that in your affirmations and prayers for manifestation, you always precede your request with the words, "if it is highest wisdom." That way you can avoid manifesting things which you may have only thought you wanted. How many times have you manifested something in your life that you thought would make you entirely happy, or would put an end to your problems once and for all? That relationship, that business, that new this or that, that new home or job — "if I could just get this" — well it doesn't work. There is always something else. Happiness lies in fulfilling your destinies. Your destinies are as Light Workers on the face of this Earth. Your destinies are involved with the ascension process at this time. This does not mean you cannot enjoy the pleasures of the worldly life while on your path. It only means that this is your ultimate goal. And by putting your focus on your ultimate goal, you accelerate your growth, as well as your ability to manifest what you desire. By surrendering to your destiny, and by giving yourself to Spirit, you accelerate your ability to manifest your needs. As Jesus said, if you seek first the kingdom of Heaven, all things will be added unto you.

The reaction you are attempting to create is instantaneous manifestation. Upon your ascension you will all be able to do this. But in the meantime, you have to raise yourselves, with our help, a little bit at time. Manifestation will not be quite so instantaneous, but you will find that it can be dramatically speeded up. It need not involve manifesting something physical. It could be an understanding or an awareness or a spiritual experience. Perhaps you have a desire to experience Samadhi, that blissful experience of union with God. This is a manifestation you can create also. Align yourselves with your higher Selves and let your desires manifest. Know that you are worthy. Know that you are deserving of your dreams. You will know which dreams are in your highest interest. If it is something which serves you, the light, and your missions, you will find it much easier to manifest.

Perhaps you have been attempting to create something in your life and it has not happened. Perhaps it is necessary for you to look at your motivation, look at the possibility that what you are trying to create is not in alignment with your mission or your true destiny. Maybe that manifestation would only act to hinder you or sidetrack you in some way. You see, it is long past the time when you can afford to be sidetracked. There may be a call that has gone forth to each of the Light Workers, to drop their extraneous activities and to manifest in alignment with their destinies. You have all heard this call, some more or less consciously. But it has affected you in a way that has caused you to have more of a desire for spiritual awakening, liberation, and ascension.

With regards to manifestation, it is necessary to have a sense of detachment, an attitude of surrender.

You may be desiring a new relationship. There is a perfect relationship awaiting you. Yet, if you attempt to force the issue in a certain situation, or with a person who is not exactly right for you, you may create a relationship which brings you a less positive experience. In fact, it may postpone your connecting with the relationship that is intended for you. So there is patience and surrender involved. I wish I could come here and snap my fingers for you and have all of your dreams come true. Wouldn't it be funny if everyone's dreams manifested instantaneously in this room? We would be able to learn a great deal about each one of you. Some of you might be a little embarrassed! You see, you are protected in this dimension, in this worldly life, from your stray thoughts and stray desires by the fact that you do not manifest instantaneously. This ability is only available to those who have mastered themselves and purified themselves, to those whose desires are totally in alignment with the light. So align yourselves with that and you will find, with some careful pruning and weeding, some careful attention to your inertia, you will attain the ability to manifest much more instantly in your lives. And this will allow you to experience more service in your lives. You can streamline your existences to be more in alignment with your true missions and destinies. The more you purify, the faster you are able to grow and be lifted.

So, at this point I would like to open the floor to questions related to self-mastery or manifestation. I would like to know what is on your minds.

"In manifestation, is it easier to get more positive results if we focus on the big picture or dream, or should we take pieces closer to the now and receive positive results with smaller manifestations and work up to larger things?"

This is an excellent question. I would say that you need to work on the small and immediate picture in the present, as well as the distant future. The manifestations that you attempt to create will be based upon your long-term goals. It is not necessary to be quite so refined or so exact in what your long-term goal is. A perfectly appropriate long-term goal is to merge with your higher Self and to fulfill your Earth mission and your ultimate destiny. This is completely open-ended you see. It can include many different types of manifestations. In fact, most of your destinies will include many different manifestations. So as a long-term goal you can have an open-ended picture. If you have a picture within you of something not quite so long-term that you would like to manifest, a lifestyle or living situation, for example, you could hold this in your mind and affirm that you are achieving this goal, even though you may feel yourself a long way from it. Then I would say, in the short term, you can have these long-term goals be your guide. You can ask in meditation, "How can I best obtain my long-term goals? What is it that I can do today? What is it that I can do in the near future? What is it that I need to manifest as a small step towards this greater goal?" Then give yourself some space to feel your guidance. When you feel guidance you will perhaps feel like changing jobs, or visiting a particular person and asking questions. It could be anything. When you get this guidance, then follow through with it, and affirm that you are manifesting your ultimate destiny one step at a time.

If you wanted to manifest a bag of marshmallows, you could sit down and meditate for hours, trying to manifest this, or you could get into your car and go to the store and purchase them. It would achieve the same end. It is also necessary for you to take part in manifestation in a worldly way. In the future, when you have attained to a more refined state, you will be able to manifest the marshmallows within your own hands. You will have that ability. But don't throw your common sense out the window! "Well, if I want marshmallows I need to get into the car and go to the store." So you need to work on both aspects.

In the small picture, common sense and practicality come more into play. In the long-term, you can be more creative and more dreamy in your pursuits. And then your practicality will align with your dream and you will find yourself manifesting practical steps towards attaining the dream. You can do this. You are a powerful being. It is often simply the power of believing that we have the ability to manifest. If you do not believe that you have the power to manifest, you have a predisposition towards sabotaging your affirmations and desires. So perhaps when you come up with a desire in your life, the first thing that you will find coming to the surface is your belief in how it is impossible for you to do that. That is where you get your gardening shears out. And you turn your back on that inertia, and affirm that you can do this, and that you can easily manifest what you desire. Call upon the ascended masters and your own I AM presence to help you to open your power centers, so that you can blast through these old emotions and false beliefs. You are all so powerful. It is time to come into alignment with your power and manifest. You are attaining to the point where all that you manifest is God's will.

"St. Germain, can you give me some guidance on how to proceed to discover and manifest my service here on Earth, prior to ascension?"

Of course. You have your long-term goal well in hand. You have aligned with your mission and your ascension process, and yet you have not created an intermediate goal. It is necessary for you to explore your desires. In your opening to be guided, you need not feel that your desires are something that need to be sacrificed. Your desires are what will guide you and give you the necessary charge to manifest. So, I would suggest for you not to be concerned about your ultimate goal for now. Know that it will manifest. Know that you are well on your way. But think about what you would like to manifest. What would be enjoyable to you? Allow yourself to dream a little bit more. Allow yourself to connect with your body, and ask your body what it would like and how it would like to live and what feels good. What feels the best to you? Perhaps this is the area you will do your manifesting in.

There is no need to feel insecure, although insecurity may come in when you feel yourself surrendering and not knowing. Fulfilling your ultimate destiny will not cause you to go hungry or cause you to be in lack. In fact, aligning with your spirit will increase your prosperity. Though your faith is being tested, also. It may not be easy, but it is all in alignment with your growth, with what is required of you. You will all be tested more. As you attempt to fully give yourself to your ascension path, perhaps you will find yourself tested a little bit more severely. Nothing you cannot accomplish, but enough to prepare you for what is to come. You will learn what you need to learn in order to assume the responsibility of the service you will perform. If your goal is smaller, then less purity and purification are required in order to achieve that. If your goal is great, then you will require more purity.

"I have a desire to help people align with their higher Selves. I wondered if you had some more information on alignment with the higher Self and how I can help others?"

First, align with *your* higher Self and radiate this experience to all that you meet. In radiating this experience of joy, love, and healing, you will attract to yourself, by your own magnetism, those who are ripe for the teachings that you have to offer. Though your teachings may be quite pure and profound, it does no good to scatter your "pearls before swine," as they say.

Your first step is to increase your magnetism: meditate, purify yourself, nurture your own garden and make it beautiful so that you may radiate this beauty to others. Then you will find yourself attracting others who have the readiness and ability to open to what you have to say. Give whatever guidance you can based upon your evolvement. Know that you are equal to all. You may have more awareness, but ultimately all beings are equal. If you maintain your humility, you may find yourself becoming somewhat of a teacher. There is a great need for teachers, and I applaud your desire to share this experience.

"Will learning to channel assist me?"

Yes, learning how to channel is a way to assist you in receiving the messages that your higher Self and spiritual guides have to give you. It is not necessary to channel in order to receive this guidance, but channeling does seem to force one into alignment and into surrendering to this more. The guidance that you receive in the form of messages and teachings from within, and from your ascended guides, will direct your attention to areas you can work on. They will assist you. Channeling is an option if you are open and if you have a desire for it. It is not necessary. You can still receive messages and guidance in meditation by asking your guides to make themselves present to you. Channeling is similar to this except it is a more refined process. It requires a great deal of surrender.

"I feel the need to move away from the city, but I'm not sure if that is in alignment with my service. I'm waiting for a sign or indication that it is okay."

Do not be afraid to make a wrong move. Do not be acting or not acting out of fear. I would say you need to come into alignment with your feelings, and if you are wondering if this desire is in alignment with your higher Self, then ask. Imagine yourself in a different environment, one that you feel more happy with. Take a few steps in that direction and see what you feel like. Perhaps you will miss the spiritual family that you have here. Perhaps you will enjoy the solitude, or create another spiritual family elsewhere. There is a leap of faith required either way you go, for neither path is perfect or totally satisfying. You will have to have somewhat of a balance in your life. It is natural to hesitate a bit because you do not wish to make a mistake, but don't be afraid to make a tiny mistake if it serves in the long run to show you your path.

We will not give you detailed guidance, for it is part of your path to make these decisions. The decisions you make reflect your alignment and your readiness to proceed on the ascension path. There is only a little time left, and you have to make maximum use of it by making the best choices you can in the days to come. We cannot rob you of your choices. We can only give you our love and a bit of guidance and reassurance. More and more it will be this way, and you will not require external answers. More and more you will know by your own intuition and by your internal guidance. This is our goal and, in fact, we are pressing you a bit in that direction.

⇝ Six ⇜

Choices

HILARION

Hello. Thank you for coming this evening. It is a pleasure for me to be here with you, sharing my energies. My name is Hilarion. I believe this is the first time I have spoken to this group, so I will introduce myself to you energetically throughout the course of the evening. And you may introduce yourselves to me by being yourselves.

Tonight I would like to speak to you about the manifestation of this New Age you are experiencing. I would like to speak specifically regarding choices that you have at this time, options that are available to you, and of the responsibility each of you have in your own choices and in the generation of experience. At this time there is great empowerment in the energies of manifestation. What once may have taken some time to create now can be manifested much more quickly. This is due to the fact that the energy and the power of grace which are coming through now are bringing the Earth into more of an alignment with Spirit. The Earth is attaining to her ascended state. In the ascended state all creation is spontaneous. There is no time lapse between the moment that you desire to have something and the time that you create it. So as the Earth is entering this new growth spiral, the power of manifestation is increasing. Perhaps you have seen that you have more power now to manifest that which you desire. You also have more power to manifest that which you do not desire. And this is what I would like to speak to you about this evening, your choices and the responsibilities inherent within consciousness and attention.

It is a time of miracles. It is a time when you can, by the choices that you make in your day-to-day experience, create a life of miracles for yourself. I would like to state that from my perspective, what you have referred to as miracles are simply the fundamental natural laws of the universe, the laws of creation and manifestation. There was a time upon this planet when manifestation was instantaneous. Beings had not lost their connection to Spirit, so they could manifest spontaneously that which they desired. Those days are returning. I am here to tell you that you are creating in each moment, especially each time you have a desire or place a projection out into the universe. They may be called miracles, or they may be considered natural laws of manifestation. However you look at them, I think it is an opportunity to choose wisely in that which you desire to experience in your lives at this time — and I accentuate the word "wisely."

Every day you make choices. Every time you direct your attention in some particular direction, on some particular thought or feeling, you are making a choice. You are giving energy to that manifestation. Your attention is the energy which makes it blossom and grow into a full experience. So each day, throughout your day, you are creating. You are choosing. And each day you choose what you will experience in that day and what you will experience in the days to come. By your conscious or unconscious choices you reap your own rewards, you reap your own manifested creations. So I am going to present to you what I would consider to be some wise choices. These are, of course, my own opinions based on my own experiences. Your own experience is your teacher. Perhaps you can take these words to heart and see if they seem true for you also.

I would feel that it is wise to choose love over hate, to choose peace over confusion and chaos, to choose abundance over lack, to choose freedom and liberation over enslavement and bondage. These are some of your options at this time. I would say that in any particular area of your life you have these choices. In the area of your spiritual growth it is most important that you are clear about what you desire, what you desire to experience and the direction you would like to go. Would you choose enlightenment and ascension? This is your primary choice at this time. All other choices are secondary to that. That choice involves the very definition of what you call life, what you intend life to be for you. Your life can be one of liberation and peace, of love, fulfillment and purpose. It can be free from confusion. It can be free from lack. It can be everything that you have dreamt it could be. In fact, it can be much more than that. It is rather impossible to dream to the magnitude of the opportunities that are now available to you. Unless you can remember what it feels like to be an ascended being, you may have a difficult time dreaming of how it feels. But if you will allow yourselves an opening in your dreams and in your desires, and give yourselves to highest wisdom and the unfoldment of growth in your life, that will be your ultimate experience.

So it is a time to make some refinements in your projections, in your thoughts and feelings. It is not a time to simply sit back and wait and see what is going to happen. Or let me say, you can, but you are also making a choice in so doing. Not choosing is also a choice. If you do not choose to create consciously in your lives that which you truly desire, you will reap the rewards of other creations. Perhaps they will be someone else's creations imposed upon you because of your lack of clarity and decision. I'm sure this is not what you desire. We are going beyond this stage. In the past age there was a great deal of disempowerment. In fact, it has been the way of the world for some time, that beings have felt they were at the mercy of other's desires and creations and that they were not powerful enough to create for themselves what they would have preferred. Those days are ending. It is up to you to end them. As you end them for yourselves individually, then they will end.

So it is a good time to acknowledge your own powers, acknowledge your own presence. Attune to this in your meditations and in your spiritual practices. Attune to the power that is within you, the power that emanates through your own chakras, the third chakra specifically. But always in alignment with the heart chakra, and allowing for the perfect balancing of all of your energy centers. Empower yourselves to be liberated and to be free and to create that which you ultimately desire. Often when you are presented with this possibility there is a little bit of confusion. Most people on this planet are not accustomed to opening to the possibility that they can have whatever they desire. When presented with that possibility they have no idea what it is they truly desire. They are not in communication sufficiently with their higher Selves to be able to receive the intuition and guidance they have been intended to receive, which is intended to reveal their purpose. Your purpose is intended to come exclusively from within you.

So if in my presenting these options to you, you have the feeling that you do not have a clear picture of what you would ultimately like to experience, I will tell you how to connect with that. Simply call upon your higher Self and the spiritual masters, whatever guides you are working with. You may call upon me, of course, and I will be with you. Ask for impressions, dreams, pictures, thoughts or feelings — however you receive — about what you would most like to experience, or concerning your purpose. Generally your purpose is quite aligned with what you enjoy, so it is simply feeling what you most enjoy and creating a way to manifest that in a way that feels complete to you. I tell you, this is critical now. It is past the time when you can remain seated on the fence wondering whether or not the New

Age will manifest, or whether or not you will give your-self to this or that. It is time for you to make your choices. Most of you have chosen spiritual growth or you would not be here tonight. This is the number one priority in your life and in doing this you open the door to many other choices and many other options for yourselves. Let me call them service opportunities. But it is time to choose, time to open to these new possi-bilities of manifestation, new possibilities that what you have believed about this physical reality is not entirely true.

In fact, the old reality and security that you have believed in are changing and transforming before your very eyes. And it can feel, if you are not anchored firmly in your higher Self, a little disarming at times. We are used to certain solid truths. It is a time when even the solid truths are changing. They are ascending right out from under us. They are all assuming higher aspects as well, as you are, as the Earth is. So truly, it is a time of great celebration and joy. We have waited a long time to bring you these messages of hope and imminent transformation. In the past we have told everyone to be patient and practice their spiritual growth and medi-tation and give themselves to the light. Now we can be a bit more imminent with our projections, for truly the floodgates have opened and the energy of the Creator is being broadcast through this planet and through every cell of your bodies. In fact, even your cells are ascending. Your cells are making some choices now. I would suggest that you attune yourselves to them and ask whether they would like to give themselves to the aging and death experience or to choose the option of growth, ascension, and immortality.

So you can see that the times that are upon you are rather incredible. They are special. This time has not occurred before. Despite all the past enlightened civilizations on this planet, the amount of spiritual energy and light that is existing and growing now has never been here to this degree before. Even the opportunity to hear this discussion and to consider the option of ascension in this lifetime is very rare. Open yourselves to the possibility of creating liberation for yourselves, the full manifestation of everything you desire, and all that is in alignment with higher purpose. It is time now. You can have this. This is my message for the evening, and it is one I am extremely happy to transmit. If you wish, you can choose to indulge in negativity, anger, and fear. You can choose to indulge in thoughts of revenge or other less evolved aspects of the mind. If you do so you will be creating instantaneously those experiences in your own bodies and consciousness. You literally have the opportunity now to make yourselves quite ill if you so choose. Or to heal yourselves. In fact, healing is the order of the day.

So my guidance for you this evening is intended to give you some feeling of control over your own experience. You are not in charge of the universe by any means. You are not even in charge of the planetary consciousness. Yet you can be quite a bit more powerful than you have been in your manifestations. You can master yourselves, master your own projections, create liberation for yourselves, become ascended masters, and perhaps even help to liberate a few others along the way

— all by being natural and by being yourselves. I think you will find that it takes a great deal of energy to create that which is not in alignment with God's will. It takes much less energy to create that which is in alignment. So if you feel that in certain areas of your life you are swimming against the current, perhaps you could take a look at the direction you are swimming. Maybe there is an opportunity for you to make a subtle shift in consciousness or awareness or in direction. I am not saying that the path of liberation is without challenge. In fact, it is quite challenging, even with all of the grace that is flowing at this time. Anyone here who has given themselves to the path has experienced, and can attest to the fact, that their own creations are facing them every day. And they are forced to accept responsibility for them. So there are no shortcuts to self-mastery. Yet, if you begin to assume full responsibility, you will become masters.

So now is the time when you can go from darkness into light, dramatically. You can make quantum leaps in your spiritual growth and in your consciousness. Time is not the factor it once was. It is becoming less of a factor each day. It is becoming more and more slippery and pliable. You can work with it and sculpt it. You can use this new energy. It is easier now, probably easier than it ever has been, once you have given yourself to it. For those who refuse to give themselves to alignment with the will of the Father, times will be more difficult. Ultimately, they will find it extremely difficult maintaining any semblance of peace. That is why I am telling you to choose and to choose wisely. Give yourselves to the joy and love. Do not choose limitations. Do not choose to honor beliefs which no longer serve you. Choose beliefs which are a little bit more of a stretch for you. Believe in yourselves, and in your ability to have what you desire. This is what we honor as we address you. We are honoring that part of you which is desiring to reach up a little bit higher, to attain more grace and light, to release density.

So what are the rewards of doing this? I know you all need motivation. It is the nature of existence that one will make choices based on what they perceive the rewards of each choice to be. I say to you, the rewards of choosing spiritual growth and surrender to God are absolutely astounding at this time. Completely astounding. You have referred to miracles and I think that you will all be doing miracles in a short time. But I think you will also feel at that time that you are simply being natural and enjoying yourselves. If you happen to create out of the etheric energies a beautiful piece of amethyst, for example, or any other manifestation which astounds and amazes those around you, I think you will do it out of being your natural self, out of desiring to serve and experience love. And it will not be such a miracle to you. There are spiritual laws which you can learn and which you will receive training in. They will allow you to understand how to perform miracles, how to be totally liberated from third-dimensional bondage to materialism and all of its limitations.

So, these are but a few examples of why I encourage you to give yourselves. And I encourage you to give yourselves by meditating, by being with your own breath in silence. I would say a couple of times a day, morning and evening are good, but also throughout your day whenever you feel a space, give yourselves to that inner peace. In giving yourselves to the inner peace you, open the door for guidance to come through, and for more presence and more power. This enhances your own power of clarity and makes things a lot easier. It makes your choices easier, makes you aware of what you are choosing and how to maximize your experience of Spirit, how to channel the light in new and exciting ways. So, if you give yourselves in meditation it will give you more clarity concerning your choices. You will observe with more awareness what you are creating. You will see the connections between your projections, between what you put your attention on, and what you experience. And once you have this awareness, it will be extremely easy for you to drop things from your lives that are no longer serving you, or that have been limiting you.

You need to have the awareness of the connection between the cause and the effect. This is where meditation and awareness come in. Aside from the fact that it can make you feel as if you are swimming in a pool of love, it also has the additional benefit of increasing your awareness of the laws of manifestation. So be in this love, and love one another. Be aware of the service you can provide simply by giving from your heart. Have any of you questions for me this evening? I offer myself to you in this way.

"I have a question about miracles. How do we attune to this? It sounds like a fifth-dimensional power and here we are in the third dimension."

Who says you are limited to the third dimension? I think you are transcending this. There is a way that you already know of to experience aspects of fifth-dimensional reality and beyond. The fifth dimension is overlaying the third and fourth dimensions. It is seeping in through the crevices and through the spaces in the atoms and molecules, and there is more light creeping in to the third and fourth dimensions. The source of this is higher than this level, so miracles can be experienced prior to your ascension and prior to the total merging with your fifth-dimensional self. You should begin by considering that miracles need not be spontaneous manifestations, but that they can take a week or two, or longer, to manifest. It could be a miracle in your consciousness. It could be a miracle in healing. It could be the experience of releasing a particular emotion or density which has surrounded you for your entire lifetime in a matter of one meditation. This is entirely possible at this time. It could be that it takes two weeks or so to release this particular experience. Nevertheless, it is still a miracle. Or shall we say, a fundamental law of physics being applied. There are many miracles already taking place. We are experiencing somewhat of a miracle here this evening. We are having a transmission or conference with an ascended master. This is somewhat of a miracle. Yet the Earth has not yet fully attained to the fifth dimension.

So more and more the fifth dimensional realms will be contacting you and coming through. And the various ways they come through tend to leave behind a presence, or a manifestation, which might be viewed as miraculous. This can be in healings. It can be manifestations of physical things. So open yourself to your desires. Place this desire in your meditations. Create some sort of pedestal and say, "Okay, I'm going to try and create a miracle in my life. I would like to take this particular emotion, or this particular ailment which has been affecting me, and put it on this pedestal and call upon guidance and ask that it be released." And see what happens. The more you can elevate yourself into fifth dimensional consciousness, the faster the materialization of these miracles can occur. Also, you must be attentive to your projections and maintain a positive viewpoint as to the outcome. If you surround your projections with doubt, they will be much less likely to manifest. So you have to suspend your disbelief a little bit with regards to creating miracles in your lives. First you have to open yourself up and say, "I'm going to believe in this even though there is part of me that does not believe in this. I'm going to believe in it anyway." You have to play with your consciousness a little bit. This is not being dishonest. This is being hopeful. This is stretching yourself.

"Can you explain your focus?"

My focus is speaking to you! I am focused upon the moment that I am in, and so I am also able to be rather flexible in my manifestations. I will say that I am especially effective in the areas of inspiring trust and faith, in transmuting doubts and fears. In my lifetime as Saint Paul I learned a great deal of humility, which I have not forgotten. So if you are desiring to know how I can help you, I would say call upon me and see how I feel to you. If you are feeling an area of doubt arising concerning anything, yourself or your own spiritual path, or whether there is such a being as God, call upon me and I will assist you in understanding. I am one who would come and strengthen you in times of need. Also, I am very much enjoying my channelings at this time, through the various beings I am coming through. I am very expressive and I enjoy expressing myself in speech. Despite its limitations, I have a great deal of fun speaking. If you call upon me I will speak to you, and then it is for you to be able to attune yourself to hear me.

"Can you share with us on emotional transmutation?"

I think you are feeling this in your life, are you not? As a prerequisite to the ascension, or spiritual liberation, it is necessary to refine your aspect and to release densities that you have accumulated surrounding your emotional bodies. You have to release what has clung to your emotional bodies. You have been here for many lifetimes and you have had many experiences. Many of them have been quite intense emotionally. All of the experiences that you have ever had have been impressed upon your emotional body. Many of them you have released in previous incarnations. Many of them you have released in this lifetime. Some of them you have yet to release. It is necessary, in order that you attain to the lightness and to the higher frequency of vibration that is required for liberation, that you allow these experiences to be transmuted. Allow yourself to feel and experience them as they are leaving you.

So what happens when someone gives himself to the ascension process is that your vibrational frequency begins to rise gradually, and as it does, the density within your emotional body can no longer exist at that frequency. So it must be released. So the very fact that you are giving yourself to spiritual growth is resulting in your emotional release at this time. This is part of the process. It is something that you need to do consciously, by feeling. You will feel them as they are departing. After they have departed you will feel lighter, more free and expanded. So this is perhaps the number one manifestation of the transformation that is occurring now. This is where it is felt most dramatically by human beings. For human beings have come to this planet, to this sphere, to learn love and the higher emotions, like the emotion of devotion. So all of these emotions will be purified and you will have only left within you those that are positive and beneficial and able to coexist in the higher frequency of Spirit. This is a rather general answer to your general question.

Self-mastery does require that you gain some control over your creations. This includes your emotional creations. Nevertheless, even if you were to one hundred percent, create only positive emotions from this day on, you would still have to process what you have already created. So, assume responsibility for those aspects of yourself which are coming to the surface now to be cleaned out, to be released. Bless them and feel them. You must feel them one more time. You felt them going in and you must feel them going out. Everything you have accepted into you as a reality. Do not accept other people's creations. Accept only your own positive creations. It is in your power to do this. It is not something that requires a great deal of psychological training. It is something that you will feel as time goes on. All will be released. Sometimes it is helpful to know the origin of your emotional process and sometimes it is unnecessary. Sometimes it is simply something that is left over from other lifetimes. Have trust and know that you are never given too much to deal with at any one time. Your guides are monitoring your process. So though it may feel that you are overwhelmed at times, this is not true. You may be taken to the 99th percentile of your ability to deal with it, but never over the top. It is not our intention to cause you to grow so fast that you are damaged by emotional discharge. This is why time is of the essence. I came through this evening to talk about choices. Now is the time to choose, because all of your unfinished business is coming up to be cleared. The less unfinished business you have, the better off you are. And the longer time you give yourself to clear it, the easier it is also. So begin now, because you have no way of knowing how much longer you have in the third-dimensional reality.

So, I think that it is time for me to go. I have enjoyed speaking with you, speaking this language which is so elusive. I am mastering it more and more each day. I have gone beyond the point of frustration to the point of playfulness. So if I use a wrong word occasionally you must forgive me. Know that what my purpose is in coming is to shower my emanation of love and healing. You are welcome to return at any time, as this is an open forum. There are many other beings who would like to speak with you and who could benefit from these interchanges. So I invite you to invite them. Your presence has been quite beautiful this evening, and I hope you have enjoyed yourselves as much as I have. Until we meet again, good night.

⤳ SEVEN ⤳

Grounding The Light

ASHTAR AND WOTANNA

Welcome. Good to see you here this evening. This is Ashtar. Tonight I will be bringing you something a little bit different, and perhaps we will even have a second speaker. We will be doing some work this evening, something very powerful for your well-being. We'll be bringing in and anchoring your light bodies a little bit more deeply into your physical forms. We will be working to empower you more, to open your lower chakras. You have gotten accustomed to working from the heart up, but tonight we are going to take it to a deeper level. This will help to align and expand you in a more balanced way. With balance you can accomplish all that you desire. You can be empowered, you can be powerful manifestors and be more grounded in your lives. This will result in more physical health, more mental and emotional health, and a great many benefits. The work we will be doing this evening is quite important.

Relax. Don't forget to breathe. Stay attuned as you are listening. This is how to achieve the maximum benefit from this gathering. There are many beings here. Many physical beings and many more non-physical beings, so this is somewhat of an orchestrated gathering. Those of us who are in higher dimensions will be assisting those of you who are still in the physical to achieve that which we have achieved — the ascension.

So here you are, all of you beings of light, Starseeds, Light Workers. You have been on this planet for a long time, as you know, many lifetimes. Yet you are not strictly of this dimension — you are from higher realms. And you share many things in common. Your mission overall is one and the same. You also share other experiences and one of these is a tendency to have an aversion to becoming fully grounded in the physical plane, to manifesting with full power and intensity within the physical form. There is a tendency among you to wish to remain in the higher centers, to avoid contact with that which you may feel more dense.

Let me give a little historical perspective. When you first incarnated here, you came as Light Workers, as spiritual beings who came to assist humanity in uplifting and raising the planetary consciousness. You came as teachers and examples. We might call you radiators of light and love and Spirit. And yet when you came here, the density of the experience — the negativity, anger, fear and all of the lower emotions prevalent on this planet — were a shock to your systems. Many of you have not yet fully recovered from that shock. Others tended to fare better. And this experience, this reaction to being present in the physical form, has been carried in various ways through many lifetimes. And now that you are awakening more and more to your spiritual presence, to your purpose, there can be an even greater tendency on your parts to desire to escape into Spirit, to expand in a direction you might feel is "higher."

It is true that it is your path in this lifetime to raise your frequencies and your consciousness, to experience the ascension, to elevate your physical forms into the higher dimensions from which you came. So your beliefs in this regard are based upon truth. Yet the very experience of not being fully present in your bodies has resulted in more difficulty here than is necessary. In fact, it is somewhat of a hindrance to your being ascended or lifted. We desire to lift you totally. We do not wish to receive only your heads! It is necessary, in order to become an ascended master, to have fully functioning limbs!

All of you have subconscious memories of your first incarnation, and of all of your subsequent incarnations in the physical form. And having been here and having experienced a great deal of the pain and discomfort that you have had to bear in your many lifetimes, there is a natural aversion to getting in any deeper than you need to be. You like to dip your toes a bit into the water rather than plunging fully into the physical form. And yet, what the higher Self is requiring of you now is to manifest fully, through every level of your being. In fact, you could say that many of the problems you have encountered in your life are due to your not being fully present within your physical form, to not being balanced in all of your centers. If you have not brought yourself down fully into the body, into your power centers, it is very difficult to have anything but an experience of powerlessness. If you are having difficulty manifesting that which you desire, financially or other ways, this is also an indication that you need to work more on bringing the energy in and empowering yourself. There is a great deal of power within the body when Spirit is fully integrated. You are intended to be able to create what you desire easily, with much less stress. You are intended to have an experience of security and peace. Yet if you are not fully present in the physical form, there will be a tendency towards fear and towards feeling abandoned. There will be a feeling of disconnection from Source.

In fact, when you first came to this planet as volunteers, one of your initial reactions, in many cases, was the feeling of shock at how it all felt so different. It is very different to be within the third dimension compared with the fifth dimension. And part of this shock over time created the sense of having lost your connection with your source, with the ships, with your original points of origin. And that feeling of being abandoned, of being cut off, has resulted in feelings of distress and powerlessness, fear, anxiety. And many of you have spent many lifetimes being very humble, very meek in your mannerisms. Though you came here to be powerful beings of light, you often found yourselves clinging to a lesser experience. This is not to say you have not done your spiritual work — you have. This is not a criticism. It is merely a fact. And now as you are awakening, those tendencies that remain within you to be meek and fearful and powerless still cling to you, still have a strong hold upon your subconscious memory and your emotional bodies. What is needed to heal this and to restore you to full presence is a full blast from your Spirits, manifesting through your entire being and radiating and transmuting those old ideas and concepts once and for all.

Whenever you feel yourself fully aligned and connected with Spirit there is no fear. There is peace and love. There is trust. But you see, there has been a tendency, when confronted by fear, to attempt to escape. And escape for you has often meant an attempt to return to Source through higher centers, leaving the body behind. You have attempted to leave your bodies to avoid confrontation and pain. So there remains a strong ingrained tendency here that we are going to work with.

You will benefit from being here fully. Even if you consider yourself on the ascension path, waiting for the first wave to lift you so that you can return to your natural state, you are still here now. And you must still live and cope with this reality as you are ascending and becoming more enlightened. The process requires that you be fully empowered within your body, that you love yourself fully, not only the part of yourself that you consider spiritual. Love the body and allow this love to penetrate every cell and heal you. Let yourself feel the connection with the Earth, which is a tremendous source of strength. Part of the work that you need to do is to become fully present so that you can channel more energy through your bodies in your various services, and also into the Earth for the healing of the planet.

So if you are wondering why at times you are having difficulty experiencing higher states of consciousness, or bringing more energy in, perhaps you need to look at your grounding. You can only absorb a certain amount of spiritual energy if you are not an open conduit allowing it to flow through. It will become stagnant if it does not flow through you. And one of the ways it longs to flow through you is through your legs into the Earth, to connect you with the Earth so that you can feel more smoothness in the flow of energy. If you have experiences in meditation or your channelings of feeling a little bit "over-amped" this is due in large part to not being fully grounded. When you are grounded you can bring through vast amounts of energy, vast amounts of spiritual presence, and not feel overwhelmed by it. Of course, there is a tendency to feel stretched from time to time. You can greatly relieve the intensity of this by being more grounded in the physical.

As you know, this New Age is upon us. It is manifesting very powerfully. You are all experiencing the increase in light energy. Your bodies are attempting, in whatever ways they can, to open to this energy. You will need to release the blocks and open the areas where you are constricted so that you can handle this new inflow of energy in a peaceful and natural way. Every day you are receiving more. Every day your bodies are being called upon to transmute a little bit more, to become bit lighter, to vibrate a little bit faster, to raise the frequency of vibration. And this goes for your legs too, not just for your heart and crown. It is for your entire body. You are one package. Your head will not function very effectively if it is vibrating at a faster rate than your legs. This creates discomfort and headaches. So open yourselves to this process and to breathing more from your bellies. Let the breath flow all the way through you. Let it expand your lower chakras. Be relaxed. This brings the energy more into your body and is very healing.

What is the best way to escape duality and limitation? It is to ascend, to achieve enlightenment and liberation. Yet the enlightenment and liberation that you will achieve, will be not brought about by your dying and leaving the physical body, but by ascending with your physical bodies into the higher realms, to meet your teachers face to face. This is why you need to be open fully.

So I think it is time to call forth another who would like to speak with you. This is one who is an expert in this area, and who is also quite a character! We will meditate a little bit, and hopefully we can bring him in to be with you to continue this process.

Hello. My name is Wottana. I am best understood by you as a Native American. My last lifetime was in a tribe called the Sioux. For many centuries, thousands of years, my tribe were the caretakers of this land. My tribe, meaning not only the Sioux tribe, but all Native Americans. We lived in communion with the Earth Mother, yet our source is, as yours is, in the stars. One thing we mastered was being grounded, being one with the Earth. We knew how to be strong, how to be spiritual warriors.

We are the tribes who have been aligned with the Father's energy. Most of us are no longer in physical bodies. For the intensity of the Earth's vibration, the negativity and density, the fear and anger, became too strong for us. So we departed to other realms where we, too, have been awaiting this time. Now that it is here we are doing all that we can to help.

So I have been invited by Ashtar, by the "space men" as you call them, to come and assist you in grounding, to open you up a little more to the wonder of your own physical body, to the joy that comes from being on the Earth. You have need to experience the joy and presence. You have need to connect to the Earth, to love the Earth and allow your spirits to come through your bodies and touch the Earth. Most of the time you are walking around in your heads. You use your body to carry your head around! Your head is very important, but it is not everything. Living from your head alone makes you crazy!

Now you are trying to bring more Spirit into your bodies. You are trying to open your hearts. I warn you, when you open your heart you are opening to your full presence, for the heart will love not only your head but your whole self. So now it is time to take it a little deeper. We will do what we can this evening to help you. In fact there are many here with me. Many of my tribe. Though we have not been incarnated in bodies for some time, we have been working. We have been guiding, assisting those who leave their bodies in death, guiding them. We have been carrying messages, giving you messages, sending you healing energy.

So open to our presence. Now is the time. Use all the resources at your disposal. Tonight we present you with another resource — Wottana. When you call upon me I will help you. If you are afraid I will help you. If you are in your head I will come and laugh at you! You are not enjoying yourselves enough in your bodies. You are waiting to get out of your body. You are waiting to ascend, and you think if you ascend you will not have to deal with your bodies. You've got to take your body with you. You've got to do some healing down here. You've got to learn to love yourselves physically as well as spiritually. Take care of yourselves. When you withhold the energy of Spirit from your lower chakras, from your lower centers, you break the flow of energy. You break the flow of light force. This results in illnesses. It results in imbalanced emotions — all sorts of feelings.

Beautiful people like yourselves, you should not be suffering any more. You should be happy. Even though you are waiting to ascend, you should enjoy your physical forms. I tell you, when we were here we enjoyed our physical forms. We took great pleasure, great joy, for we did not feel the Earth was separate from the Creator.

All is one. So your body is divine too. Don't be so fast to escape from it. Enjoy it. I am looking forward to taking another body, but I will not do so under these conditions. The world is too crazy for me. I will come back when all is clean and purified. When the crazy ones are gone. Then I will dance on the plains. I will get a new body, the same as you.

I'll give you some tips tonight. I know you like to get tips so you can ignore them! You get so many tips you don't know what to do with them. Everybody has got advice. Well, I'm no different. I will give you some advice about how to be happy being here, how to enjoy your physical presence and heal yourselves. Then you can become the powerful warriors that you are. When you are powerful, when you are fully present in your bodies, the negative energies cannot harm you so much. Then you are solid and strong. You have protection. You are not afraid. You don't have to avoid crazy humans.

So how to bring the energy down? Number one, I'll say it one more time. When you do your meditation and you are breathing, and even when you are doing your work, always breathe from down here in your stomach area. Bring it down all the way. You notice when you are afraid, the first thing you try to do is to get out of your body. You try to get out and you don't breathe. This makes you powerless, and then you are more afraid. What you should do when you are afraid is to come more into your body. Ground yourself into the Earth. That brings in the strength and then the wisdom. If you are trying to get out of the top of your head it is difficult to hear your guides and your body telling you what to do. If you are pulling the energy down into your bodies you are also pulling down the wisdom. You bring your guides into your body for more protection. You are very powerful beings and you have a lot of allies. Very powerful allies. You've got to learn to use them and trust them and let them come in all the way. So breathe down here. Practice it. When you do this you can call on me or any of the others. Some members of the tribe will be sent to you. It is our specialty. You call on me. I will be with you to make you strong, to make you feel happy. More energy, strength and healing. More power in your body. More power in your manifestation. More power in your speech.

The light wants to be in every cell. When you restrict the light from your cells you wreak havoc on your own bodies, you create imbalance. So breathe and call upon me. Practice it when you are walking in the woods, and I will walk with you. Native Americans are your friends, especially those of us who are like you, Starseeds. We know what it feels like to be here. So we can help. We want to get the show on the road. We are tired of waiting, too.

I'll give you another hint. Say you are walking down the street or in the woods. Let's say that you have a brilliant realization that you are being crazy, that you are thinking and worrying and you are in your head too much. When you are like this you can't even feel your body or legs. You are like robots. When you feel that way, when you realize you are a little bit lost, walk along and feel your feet upon the earth. If you can feel the sensation of your feet it will pull your energy down into your bodies. This is a great trick. This is why it is good to go barefoot sometimes. You can really feel the Earth when you are barefoot. Find a place where there is dirt under your feet and try it then. Wiggle your toes in the dirt and ask for Wottana to be with you. There will be many rewards. You open yourself and you can manifest better. You get more power. Ideas come from here (head). But you give them the power from here (lower body). It is very strong. There is a martial art called aikido. They use this (lower body power center). They come from down here. And you can't knock them over.

Do you have any questions for me? If I can help you I will.

"Since I was young I've always had delicate health and allergies. Is there anything you could share with me that could strengthen my immune system and increase my health?"

That's what we are working on now. You have a lot in common with others here. You come here, light beings, manifesting in a world of darkness. You are bound to get some challenge and difficulty. So what you do is you try to get out. You try to be here as little as possible. You have resistance to being fully in your body. This results in fragile health. It makes your nerves a little bit more sensitive. You have got to be fully present. Bring the energy in using the tips I am giving you. Call on me. I would be happy to help you. I think

you have some Native American energy in you some-
where. It is easier to help you, the more Native
American lifetimes you have had. I think you have all
had some. So connect with that part of you. Connect
with that warrior spirit and come down into your body
fully. Let the energy circulate and flow through. That
will help a lot. Just remember that nothing is perfect
here. You will feel better, more energy. You'll radiate
more. Then you get like a protective shield. Maybe your
shield gets strong enough that pollen can't even come
in. I'll bring you some medicine men.

I work to open up the downstairs. Other guys work
to open the upstairs. Together we get your house in
order. And energy comes from the stars and goes into
the Earth and heals the Earth. Mother Earth is crying
and we are doing what we can. You do what you can.
If you heal yourself, you also heal the Earth. If you heal
yourself, you heal somebody else by touching them, by
looking at them. Call on us Native Americans. We're
flying all over the place. We have ponies now with
wings. Everybody is busy, waiting on you hand and
foot. You've got to learn to be happy and enjoy yourselves. Don't worry so much about what's up here in
your head, ideas, thoughts and confusions. Be here in
this body, then go to the other dimensions. You can
have Ashtar tell you about the eighth dimension. Big
deal! You've got to feel it. You have to go there yourself. It's like if you are walking across the plains and it's
110 degrees and you are thinking of water. Just thinking about it doesn't help, does it? So don't worry about
the eighth dimension; it's doing fine without you.

"I was told that I'm actually holding something in my third chakra, something that I associated with hurting people. I was wondering how I would do what you ask."

The same way. You've all been here many lifetimes. But you did things. Maybe you judged yourselves. You felt that maybe you misused your power, so you decide never to use it again. Either that, or you came through in a powerful way to teach these people something, and then they hurt you. So you said to yourselves, "I'm never doing that again. I'm going to keep it to myself. I'm going to be meek and humble." You did this to stay alive. So all of you have a lot of power here that is sort of stagnant and needs to come out. You are holding it in. You're waiting until it is safe. Find a safe place and let it out. You have a fear that if you let it out into the world others are going to look at you funny. Or that if you become a spiritual warrior, everyone will be coming to you and asking you crazy questions like you are asking me tonight! Except you have to stay here! I can go back where I came from and sit around the campfire and smoke the pipe.

Maybe the power doesn't want to come out because you have judgments about yourself, and criticism and fear. You don't have to worry any more. If you let your power out now, what you release will be with the light. It's going to carry the light and make you radiate more. It's going to radiate outward in a healing way. Then you'll be able to manifest more too. Don't have that fear that you would hurt someone if you let it out. You can be a spiritual warrior. Spiritual warriors never hurt anyone. But they don't take it either. Learn how to stand up for yourselves. Don't let them blow you away with their craziness. Learn to stand still. When you are confronted, connect with the Earth and feel your feet and feel your power. You can be like a boulder that is in the stream. The water flows all around it, but it doesn't move. It's not going anywhere. Be like that about this world, about your thoughts and other people's thoughts and judgments. Just let it flow around you. You don't have to move. You don't have to get out of the way. Let them get out of your way. You are the ones that know the truth. Don't be afraid. You won't hurt anybody. Now you can release yourself from your vow, all of you. Release yourself from those ideas you had. Maybe you did hurt somebody. So what. We've all made mistakes.

You all have protection around you. You all have guides working with you. They are waiting on you hand and foot. Whatever you want, you can ask them and they are there. This is a very special time. Sometimes you don't feel them, but still they are there. Sometimes you don't feel them and it makes you cry. Sometimes you have to cry. You've got to feel those emotions. Sometimes you feel the sorrow from being here in this body for so long, and you feel the pain of it, like angels stuck in a body. Don't be afraid to feel it. Anchor yourself. Ground yourself. If you are grounded it won't blow you away. You won't be afraid of it and you can feel it then. And you can be strong. When you feel it, it goes away and doesn't come back and you get clear. Then you bring in more light. Then you get what you are wishing for all along. We'll all get it together and everybody will be happy. The power is ours now.

So, I guess Ashtar is telling me I have to meditate with all of you crazy people!

∽ EIGHT ∽

Beyond Duality

MEHER BABA

Welcome. Nice to be here with you. This is my first opportunity to address most of you. My name is Meher Baba. It is indeed an honor and a pleasure to be with you. I am tonight's mystery guest, and I hope you will not be disappointed with what I have to share with you. I think you will not.

All of us who come through and speak to you in this way are sharing, primarily, ourselves: our own presence, our own vibrational energies. Then of course, we must come up with some sort of topic to share with you, so you will not become too bored! Something to occupy your minds and your understanding, while we share the love of our hearts. So please relax, and make yourselves comfortable. I would like to speak tonight about several aspects of spiritual growth: liberation, acceptance, and going beyond duality. I think I will call my talk "Going Beyond." It has a nice ring to it.

You are all here because you are involved with your spiritual paths. You are here because you have a longing and an internal desire to experience the Creator, in whatever way you refer to that energy — whether you call it God or Higher Self, or whether you refer to it as Light or simply as Oneness. It is essentially the same desire and the same drive which bring you to these kinds of gatherings to open yourself. So, you have been involving yourselves, some of you for many years, with spiritual growth, with opening yourselves to your deepest potential, with evolution of consciousness. And I think we have a very diverse group here this evening, as usual; many different paths and many different experiences have converged in this particular moment. And I would like to speak with you about this spiritual path that you are all on and about going beyond, going all the way in your conscious awareness, all the way to liberation.

As you begin your path, you may start from a point of realization, a realization that certain feelings feel good to you and certain others do not. You may say that there is a right way to feel and a wrong way. You may say that there is good and evil, and that you are choosing to follow the path of good. You may say that there is light and darkness, and that you are choosing to give yourself to the light — many different ways of labeling the duality of human experience. And this duality serves you. It serves you in your present situation, in your present consciousness. And yet, I am here to tell you this evening that your point of completion, the point that you are moving towards in your growth, is beyond all such duality. The point where you become one with the Creator in consciousness is the point at which you have transcended all duality, and no longer do "right and wrong, "light" and "darkness" have an effect upon your consciousness. And no longer do you view the world through your current set of beliefs and understandings.

Most of you have quite a sophisticated sense of spirituality, and you know, for the most part, what is best for you. I will not tamper with this. But I would like to bring out the point that even at your current level of sophistication, you are still dwelling somewhat in a state of duality. You are still tending to view the spiritual path as choosing "light" over "darkness," or escaping darkness in favor of the light, this type of awareness. Most of you have teachers who come through and speak to you, either in your own messages, or in channelings, or in other literature. Your teachers use this very foundation of duality as the ground upon which to instruct you and to teach you, speaking as if they also believe in dualities. In fact, none of us believe in dualities. We are using this perspective only as a frame of reference. And tonight, I am chosen to come through and speak about going beyond this into direct oneness with the Creator, which is attainable. This is your goal. This is, in fact, your present condition. You see, you are all experiencing God. You are not always perceiving it as such, yet you are. No matter what you do, no matter where you go, no matter who you speak to on what subject, no matter what actions you indulge in, you cannot escape this ultimate reality, this ultimate condition. God is everywhere, or else it would not be God.

So you see, you are dwelling within an experience of oneness, attempting through the longing of your hearts to experience this oneness. Yet you are still somewhat involved with the dualities of "this is good and this is not good," this sort of thing. But, you have to go through these levels of consciousness. Obviously, it does you very little good to sit back and say to yourself, "I am one with God" and consider your spiritual path complete. You may try this and see if it is effective. I think there is more awareness to be achieved. Know that you have yet to unwind your beliefs and your programming, to come to the point of actual emergence within your consciousness, to the actual *experience* of union. This is your goal. This is liberation.

The reason why I am speaking of this, this evening, is to give you a little assistance in transcending, in going beyond your beliefs — even your beliefs about spirituality. Let me say that I am here to give you a little boost. A little boost up, through the branches of the tree that you are climbing to where your head sticks up a little bit into the sky, and you can see all around. Most of you are still climbing the tree. You are finding the proper branch to grab hold of. And when you find that proper branch, you feel "this is good, this is spiritual, this is light." And if you grab the wrong branch and fall a little bit, you say that was "bad." So, in effect, what you are doing is quite appropriate. Yet, when you have achieved the ultimate height of the tree, there will come a point where you can stick your head up through the branches and see the sky as it truly is, no longer divided by patterns of consciousness, by the leaves and the branches that you are still enmeshed in at this point.

Even now you feel, from time to time, a clear ray of that divine presence, and you know the experience of going beyond. And this is what keeps you climbing, keeps you seeking for the correct branch to grab onto, that which will support your weight, that which will allow you to rise a little bit higher in your awareness.

So, what can you do to assist yourself in going beyond? What can you do to expedite matters, knowing that you are still somewhat involved in your belief patterns about spiritual life, knowing that you still feel aversion to certain experiences and attraction to others? You still have desire. You have a desire to be one with God, which is ultimately the purest desire. You have other desires to contend with. And all of these desires are what are tending to create an experience of duality in your lives. How can you go beyond desire? How can you go beyond, to a state of total satisfaction in this moment? Total satisfaction that is not dependent upon what you are experiencing as an individual ego or physical form. Liberation is going beyond this. Even while you are in the body form, experiencing all of the sensations of third-dimensional reality, it is possible to go beyond. Beyond attachment. Beyond the need to create "good" and "evil." Beyond the need to create any more dualities.

I would say it is important to begin with acceptance. Acceptance in the sense of allowing, allowing yourself to be who you are in this moment, just as you are, without self-criticism, without labeling yourself as being in a spiritual state or not. You see, you have all categorized yourselves quite effectively, and continue to do so, even as you grow spiritually. You label your experiences. You categorize and often judge yourself if you are not feeling particularly inspired or connected. A certain day you might view yourself more negatively. I say it is important for you to begin to allow yourself to be just as you are and know that you are not separate, even though you may have the experience of separation at a certain level. You can begin to pierce this veil of illusion and have an experience of clarity.

So, I would recommend acceptance as a practical step for each of you, who are so involved in your growth, who sometimes can't see the forest for the trees. To accept is to pull back a little bit from ego identification with your experience in the moment and to merely allow yourself to be, to just feel whatever you are feeling. Allow yourselves to experience, fully, your life, just as it is in any given moment. This is an aspect of self-love. Self-love involves loving yourselves right where you are now, no matter what you feel about yourselves, or what your experiences. It is allowing yourself to be in the experience of love, regardless of your self-judgments and criticisms. It is non-resistance.

In your practice, in your meditations, how often do you get into the situation where you are labeling your experience or judging it, saying, "this meditation was not very good; this meditation was excellent"? I know this is a natural occurrence. It is natural to do this. And yet, the apparent "quality" of any given meditation experience is not an indication that you are any farther or any closer to liberation. In fact, you will attain to a point where you are no longer attached to any particular experience. At that time, you will not be so involved in your "highs" and "lows." You will transcend the "highs" and "lows" and simply be. And, in that state of being, of course, there can be an incredible sense of bliss and unity. In fact, only in that state of liberation can you achieve the maximum experience that is possible in the human form.

So what am I telling you this evening? Well, actually, I came here to confuse you! I am telling you to relax and enjoy yourselves. Enjoy yourselves as God and as manifestations of God. Try to cultivate an awareness of that oneness at all times, not merely when you are having a blissful meditation experience. God also comes to you in the form of pain. He comes to you in the form of your thoughts and confusions. He comes to you in the form of physical ailments. He comes to you in the form of carpets and trees, and telephone answering machines. Only when you are experiencing God in everything, at all times, will you be free.

There is an old saying, "Don't worry, be happy!" This is my most famous saying, and now they have made a hit record of it! It just goes to show you that good things never go out of style. And truth is truth, no matter what the format. You might say that this could be your ultimate response to my discussion this evening, to my presentation about the fact that you are somewhat enmeshed in duality, yet longing for that non-dual experience of oneness. What can you do about it? "Don't worry and be happy" is a very good place to start.

You need to connect with silence. You need to connect in meditation. For the drive that you are feeling to meditate and to, let us say, evolve yourselves, is a part of the process. I am only saying that when you have evolved yourselves, you will go beyond all these beliefs you have formulated. So don't take them so seriously. Allow for more miracles in your experience. Do not feel that if you have not meditated this morning, as per your usual custom, that you need to necessarily have a bad day or suffer all day because you did not meditate. How many of you have had this programming in your lives, on your spiritual path? And you can make yourselves quite miserable if you desire. But know that the reality is much more fluid than this. Know your spiritual practice is not intended to be something that you impose upon your sense of freedom. It is something which is designed to accentuate your experience of freedom. In other words, feel free to meditate, spontaneously, or not. If you liberate yourselves from the discipline aspect, perhaps you will find yourselves meditating even more, for you will not feel that tendency to rebel against the discipline.

You will find it quite natural, this drive within you to connect. It is very profound at this time. All of the beings who are here on this planet are experiencing it. Some are manifesting it in strange ways. Perhaps they might go out and get drunk! But they are experiencing the same inner drive for peace and satisfaction that you are. I commend you on your choice to meditate rather than to get drunk. You can get very drunk on meditation. You can and you will. You see, God has arranged it so that his presence feels very intoxicating to you. And this is something that draws you into that experience. It is simply that desire to feel the presence and the intoxication and the bliss of that loving experience of God that pulls you forward on the path. It pulls you toward reading various literatures, toward various teachers, toward channeling or listening to channelings. All of this is a direct result of the fact that God chose to make His presence feel blissful, to feel satisfying, to feel like something you have longed for, to feel like home. In fact, it is your source. In fact, you are one with it, right now. Beyond all of your strategies to enlighten yourselves, you are one with God right now.

And still, there is the need to meditate and to evolve yourselves, to evolve yourselves to the point where you have transcended your ideas about evolution. And then you can laugh at all of your strategies and all of your projections about what it would feel like to be enlightened, about what it would feel like to be liberated. I assure you it feels quite ordinary at times. At other times it feels quite blissful. It is a very fluid experience. So I would not give yourself to labeling or to projecting too strongly about what you are intending to experience. Rather, give yourself to moment-to-moment conscious awareness of your God-presence. Your own breath that is flowing through you is an excellent focus. And simply allow. Accept that which comes to you as perfect. Accept that which comes to you as God's face in disguise, coming to teach you, coming to be your guru. And make the world your guru. Make every experience, every sensation a manifestation of the God-presence it already is.

Accept. Accept it all. Try to accept it all with equanimity, with a little less passion, a little less desire, a little less desiring one experience over another, a little more simplicity. This will open the door to that which you are attempting to experience. This will open the door to that bliss and that light you are longing to merge with. It is there in your meditation where you will first experience it. And the more you can focus upon it, the more you will be — in effect — cutting through the duality, cutting through pleasure and pain, good and evil, judgments, self-criticisms. It is very simple. It is simply being with that which already is within you. Meditation is a tool that you use to, let me say, accomplish the obvious, to re-create that which is already created. So, use meditation to go beyond limitation. Do not use it to whip yourselves into a frenzy. Do not use it as a means of judging your own worthiness. Do not use it as anything other than as it was intended to be used: simply as a way and means to cut through the mental and emotional bondage of human life, to have a direct peek through the branches at the sky above. When you sit in meditation, it is like sitting in your tree at a particular spot where there is a clear ray of light coming through, right into your heart, right onto your head, and simply basking in that. Perhaps you have some more climbing to do before you can fully experience the light of the sun, yet you can take a rest, take some time to merge with that ray of the sun.

You see, when you have attained your liberation, you will experience life as a party. You will experience life as a game, and that you yourself are one of the players of the game. No separation in consciousness will exist between you and any other player in the game. You will look into the eyes of those around you and see yourself. You will see yourself as God. And you will simply be flowing, floating down the river of existence, emanating the love and presence of the Father, the Father/Mother God.

And in your emanation you will become a teacher. In my current status, I have been acting as a teacher of teachers. And I teach now the same way I taught my students when I was in physical form. I sit, and in silence, radiate my presence and my love, which is the love of the Father. I allow the Father's energy to be focused through my particular manifestation and to radiate. This is my teaching. You might think it would get boring, but it never does.

So you, yourselves, can make an ally of silence. You can merge with the silence in your meditations and gently allow yourself to drop all of your wants and desires and needs for a few moments, and simply be. Feel what you feel, and know that what you feel is God. And that feeling will grow and it will consume you. It will, in fact, annihilate you. At least that portion of you which has been keeping you in the dark, that portion of you which has kept you in the belief of separation.

So, I open the floor to your questions. Let me know what you are worrying about lately!

"I have a question about 'twin flames'. Would you speak some about twin flames and … I'm asking because I'm personally interested to know if my own is on this planet or if within my lifetime I'll have a chance to meet this person?"

I think there is a very good chance that you will meet this person in your lifetime, since you are not going to die! Let me say that the goal of human life is not to connect with your twin flame. The goal of human life is to experience enlightenment and liberation. And yet, on the path to enlightenment and liberation you will undoubtedly connect with your twin flame. Some of your twin flames are not in the physical at this time. You will meet them upon your ascension.

"Meher Baba, I have a question which might be personal, but it might help other people too. I noticed the last couple of days, Saturday and Sunday, I experienced some very intense energy. I haven't really had a chance to compare notes with other people, but sometimes I find out there are others that feel it too. It seemed when I went inward to feel it, it seemed to be somewhat connected with the desire for ascension and the ascension class where I experience so much joy and aliveness and new dedication to being in the world. It's been quite wonderful, less attachment. In fact I've had people become uncomfortable because I'm not so attached. But suddenly this weekend it felt like I got hit with a ton of bricks and just a sense of overwhelm at being here. I look around and people on the street look really gross to me and life looks really gross, and it's been really startling. Your talk on duality has helped a lot, but maybe you could say something else about this."

Yes, it has been rather intense lately, with the clearing of emotions, etc. It seems that you go through one phase and come out through the top into the clear, have a little time to enjoy it, and then you go into another clearing phase. This is the nature of growth. It comes to you in waves. So you have experienced another wave. I would not say it is personal to you, but that it is your personal reaction to the energy that is coming in at this time. It is an energy which is clearing and enlightening at the same time. It shows you aspects of yourself. It is a clarifying force. So you see parts of yourself that you had not been so aware of as the light penetrates into your crevices. And also, you are having the experience of being lifted. It is, of course, a perspective of duality to see a light and a darkness, a grossness and a beauty, and yet it is part of the path. In your lifting you are experiencing a difference between you and the mundane human consciousness. You are seeing the darkness, or the apparent darkness. You are seeing the apparent pain and suffering that all are experiencing to some degree in this would. And this is something that you have experienced also.

There will come a point when you transcend the duality, when you can see God in everyone. No matter how pitiful a specimen they may appear on the surface, you can experience the God-presence within them. And then, at that point, perhaps they can also become your teachers. What you experience in this world is a reflection of your own judgments and dualities, let me say. So, the nature of duality is that you first perceive that you are experiencing it, and then you see through it.

This is the nature of your paths at this time. First you experience that you are not connected. You are feeling a lack, some sort of separation. Even though it is an illusion, it is something that drives you forward to experience the oneness. I think you will find that the tests and the challenges become rather intense at times. But the challenge is always to transcend duality. And in order to transcend it, you must first perceive it.

So, let that experience of the grossness of the physical world be something which inspires you to go beyond it. And not in a way that you attempt to escape it in meditation, but rather in a way that you go beyond the perception of the dualities, of light and darkness, or ugliness and beauty. It has been one of your prime motivations to escape from this duality, to escape from limitation and suffering. But you see, this escape is not, in itself, based on reality. Yet it is serving a purpose in driving you into meditation so you will ultimately transcend your desire to escape. You will get to the point where you are perfectly fine. Whether this occurs after you ascend or prior, it makes no difference, the experience is the same.

So do not be self-critical about these feelings. Just know that they are part of the path and something that is there for you to experience. Try not to give too much energy to your desire to escape the ugliness, but rather, go within and accept it as it is. And accept that you will be transcending your aversion to it just as you will be transcending your attachment to beauty. What you merge with will be quite beautiful, but you will not be attached to it in the same way. There is beauty even in ugliness. There is beauty even in aspects of suffering, and all of this serves a purpose. In its purpose, it is moving you towards the experience of the Divine. This is a matter of realization, not a matter of conceptual understanding.

"I have one more question, Meher Baba. I feel like, for some time now, I've been longing to remember what I came here to do. I feel frustrated that I haven't been able to come close to any kind of a realization. Can you shed some light on this?"

Indeed, what you have come here to do is to transcend and to merge into the ascension experience, the liberation. Often times, when one experiences God, one experiences the desire to do service, to channel this energy in some particular way. And there are periods when you are feeling this energy and the desire to channel it, to serve, and yet you are not feeling a clear direction. At this time, give yourselves to the understanding that what you have come here to do may have little to do with third-dimensional reality. All of your actions of service in the worldly sphere are reflections, or by-products, of enlightenment. You are here to be a spontaneous teacher, a spontaneous channel of Divine Grace. It is not as important as you may have thought what particular manifestation you choose to create in your channeling of this energy. What is important is that you are giving yourselves to it, surrendering yourself to it, and allowing yourself to do what is highest wisdom in each moment, rather than constructing some great scenario of service for yourself. There may come a time for you when you feel more clarity about a particular course of action, a particular way of manifesting. But if you are not, I would say there is more growth to be experienced, more transcendence required. You need not concern yourself that you will not have time to do what you have come to do. What you have come to do, you are doing: giving yourself to the ascension process and manifesting as a teacher. And teachers must be rather flexible in their manifestations. It is not serving either yourself or the Creator, that you, any of you, have a very limited view of your service in this lifetime. For you have many facets to your personalities and there are many ways you can be teachers, many ways you can radiate and channel this energy to assist humanity.

So I would say for you, at this point, it is somewhat a matter of detachment from your longing to find the comfort zone of a particular service. And as you are a teacher, I would say simply accept that you are here to teach, and that you can teach in each moment by the example of your own experience of the Divine. And give yourself some leeway. Give yourself the spontaneity to teach in many different ways, whatever is appropriate. The highest teaching is often accomplished in this way. You know, the world programs you to be in achievement in a certain area, to say "I am this" or "I am that," and to be successful. I think you need to transcend all of that. I think it is for you to learn to be, and to follow your intuition, spontaneously, and see where it leads you. It will lead you to service; it will lead you to realms of teaching. So it is not for me to give you a particular plan of action. I am only here to shed a little light, as you said, on this moment of your experience.

You are all far more powerful and in control of your experience than you let yourselves believe. You are all creating, in each moment, your reality. You are creating many manifestations, partaking in many illusions, and transcending many illusions. You are like wild artists, splattering paint every which way. You are like artists who get more paint on their clothing than they do on the canvas. And when you take off your apron and hang it up beside your painting, you may see that it is a more profound artistic expression than what you were planning to accomplish. So allow yourselves to be wild and scatter the paint around. Perhaps you can get a saw and cut the floor up and hang it on the wall rather than having to clean it up! One brush stroke that comes from the experience of the Divine, that comes from the Tao, from union with God, is more profound than a great canvas of many ideas.

So, let us meditate a little bit together. I ask that in your meditations, you simply be. Accept, allow yourselves to relax, and try simply focusing upon your breath. Just pay attention to it as it moves in and out of your body. Listen to it. Feel it. If thoughts arise, simply acknowledge, and return to the focus upon your breath. You need not comment upon your thoughts this evening, you can let them drift away. If they are important, they will come back.

So let me say to you all that it has indeed been a pleasure for me to be here. The work that you are doing together is so beautiful. The emanation and the consciousness which are present in this gathering are truly blessed, and it has been a pleasure for me, a great pleasure to be with you in this way. Call upon me if you desire to feel my presence. Until we meet again, good night.

NINE

Merging with the "I AM"

ST. GERMAIN

Welcome, my friends. This is St. Germain. It is getting chilly in here, so if someone would like to close the window, they are welcome to do so. This is meant to be a comfortable affair. No need to be discomforted. Please relax yourselves this evening. I am very happy to be with you, very happy indeed.

The times are quite exciting for us. The presence upon this planet grows with each day. The presence of the light. And is it not a miracle that even this evening you should get together and combine your energies in this way, even though there is such a big football game going on. I can see now who are the football fans!

Well, last time, you had quite a visit from Archangel Michael. He spoke about that oneness, that connection that you all have, the oneness with the Divine, with Creator. And I wish to communicate a little bit more on this subject. Perhaps, a little more practical information for you. You are aware, at least conceptually, that you are one with God, one with the Creator. And yet, in your practical day-to-day lives, it is very often the case that you are feeling somewhat separate, or feeling more of the distinct ego-personality than the God-presence. This is not to criticize, this is simply stating the facts as they appear to me. Tonight I would like to give you some assistance with contacting and maintaining that contact. Some practical assistance that will assist you to feel, in a real way, your oneness.

So how is it that you can be one with the Creator and still feel separate? How is it that you are one with God and yet also a unique personality manifestation? This is one of the mysteries of creation. You could view the Creator as a mighty brilliant light or a brilliant sun, in which all is light and consciousness, in which there is no differentiation. And you could say that out of that brilliant sun many flames are broadcast. Flames which have their origin in the sun, and yet which flare out in their own beautiful, unique ways. And in essence, what I am trying to get at, is that you are those flames which have burst forth with beauty and radiance from the source, always connected to the source, and yet, each individual and beautiful. Each one unique, a unique, beautiful, brilliant manifestation or expression of that oneness. This is your I AM presence, your higher Self, your God-self, however you wish to refer to it. And that

God-self is always one with the Creator. It has been since the beginning, since you were first created, since you first burst forth from that divine sun. And you are a manifestation from that Source, you see.

You could say that there is a cord or ray of light, of beautiful light, that comes from that flame, from that essence, from that God-self, down through the various frequencies of vibration. And at each frequency it radiates a particular manifestation, until it culminates in this particular manifestation that you see with your eyes open, in the physical form, the physical body. You know you have more subtle bodies. You have your emotional bodies and your mental bodies, your etheric bodies. These are all manifestations of this same light ray as it passes through different levels of consciousness.

What we are seeking to do in our ascension path, in our path towards liberation and enlightenment, is to merge this physical embodiment along with all of your emotional and mental bodies, etc., back into the consciousness and into direct contact with that beautiful God-self, that I AM presence. You could say that this is what happens when the ascension occurs. There is a merging that takes place. You do not attain to a state where you are dissolved in the great central sun or the great light, having no more personality. You will always maintain your unique presence, your unique personality. And yet, what you will merge with is that aspect of yourself that is mysteriously one with the Creator and unique at the same time. This is the I AM presence. This is the part of you that is the most divine, you could say. The highest frequency of your self, the uttermost limit of individuation that exists for a human being.

In your meditations and your channelings and your affirmations, you are seeking to draw down the essence of this beautiful, divine, perfect presence. And you are seeking to elevate your consciousness so that there is a contact, and at that point of contact, there is divine love. There is the overflowing of divine love and presence — the God-presence that fills you, fills your body, fills all of your bodies. And this is the source of bliss. Not only is it the source of bliss, it is the source of all benefits, it is the source of all good feelings, the source of all positive manifestation in your lives. You could say it is the contact with the I AM presence which activates your affirmations and your dreams, activates the perfection you are seeking to attain. And, the more you can contact this aspect of yourself, the more powerful you are, and the more your life is a reflection of that divine love.

So, if you were to view it geographically or visually, you could say your I AM presence is hovering above you at all times. You have, some of you, seen the picture in the I AM books of the human body with the ray of light and, above that, the I AM presence. This is an actual manifestation. It is a part of yourself that you are more or less aware of, that you will be more and more aware of as time goes on. Because of your dedication and devotion to the spiritual path and your ascension, the I AM presence is drawing closer and closer to you. Especially in your meditation and channeling sessions. And your ability to interact with that aspect is becoming greater. This is how you are able to channel, how you are able to manifest miracles in your lives, how you are able to receive clear guidance, and most importantly, how you are able to express and experience divine love in your heart and in your lives. It is through the instrument of your own mighty I AM presence, your God-selves. And this is how you know God. You know the part of you that is one with God, and when you feel that union taking place, you can feel yourself merged with God. And mysteriously enough, simultaneously, you are aware that you are also a unique individual manifestation — and the two are one. This is the state of consciousness that the great saints and mystics of all time have achieved. They are within their body forms, yet they are one with God, simultaneously. And when sitting with one of these masters, you will feel that you are sitting with God. You may view that being, look into their eyes, and see the presence or feel that you are in the presence of God.

Well, this is where you are all headed, my friends, and very blissful it is indeed. So tonight, I would like to do some work with you, to assist you in your opening to this I AM presence. A little more practical advice for you in your meditations. It is my divine wish, the wish of my heart, to see all of my comrades in the physical form having the ability to experience this beauty. I am aware of the apparent difficulties with maintaining yourselves in the third dimension of reality. Believe me, I have had Earth lives, many Earth lives, and this is how I came to be able to teach in this way. And I say to you that I triumphed, by the grace of God, and attained the ascension by utilizing my own connection with the I AM presence, and by nothing else. There were no teachings necessary, as far as philosophies or religious teachings. It is only your ability to connect with your I AM self that is important in your ascension.

So you are in a situation where perhaps you are waiting for the ascension wave to begin. But I tell you, you have barely scratched the surface of what is available for you to experience. You can attain to an incredibly beautiful experience even while you are waiting for the first wave to occur. It is the divine love which enters you in your communion which gives your life meaning, which gives your life purpose, and allows you to flow through the apparent contradictions and difficulties of third-dimensional reality. It allows you to cope with the relationships in your lives, all the various apparent imperfections. Divine love is the soothing balm that you need. Especially at this time, it is the soothing balm that this entire planet needs. And the more of this divine love you can bring through your bodies, the more you will be broadcasting and channeling this love through the planet itself, the easier the transformation will be. So you see, your presence here in this dimension is acting somewhat as a lubricant to the operation that is occurring. The gears are turning, and as you know, without lubrication there is a great deal of friction.

[*Telephone rings in background*]

We have a persistent caller this evening. There is one caller that is more persistent even than this. That is your mighty I AM presence calling for your attention, daily and nightly. It is for you to pick up the receiver and focus your attention upon that aspect of yourself, this is all that is required of you. This is the only understanding that is required of you.

So, how can you facilitate this transformation? And how can you expedite contacting your I AM presence? You have been meditating, you have been doing breath meditation. Some of you have been doing light meditations and channelings. All these are wonderful. And calling upon your light body, calling upon your I AM presence, this does a great deal more.

Tonight I would like to give you another exercise to perform which will perhaps assist you. We will work upon it experientially later. I will only describe it to you at this time.

In your meditation, learn to focus above you and to feel the contact with the mighty I AM presence. If you are meditating, say, upon your breath, your concentration is in listening to the sound of your breath. Perhaps you will do this to begin your meditations and then, at a certain point, you may see light within your higher chakras. Your forehead and your crowns may become filled with light, and you will find yourself meditating on this. Or, at times, you may be able to focus upon both simultaneously. This is extremely beneficial, also. But when you have attained to an ability to meditate in this way, it is very beneficial for you to affirm for the contact with your I AM presence. Ask that your I AM presence make itself felt, ask that it descend around you. In doing so, you will actually feel the presence of your higher Self, surrounding you with light. And at that point, you can focus upward. You can perhaps open your higher chakras, your eighth and ninth chakras, a little bit. Simply focus your attention above you and you will feel a presence there. You will feel yourself extending upwards. Let me say, you will feel your consciousness extending upwards to the area high above your head, or above your head to a certain extent. You may visualize this as a beautiful ray of light coming down, or the presence of a divine ball of light or a light body, however you wish to see it. You may use the pyramid — the light pyramid — also. We have had some experience with that previously.

It is possible to maintain an awareness of your I AM presence, a sense, a feeling of its presence in your lives. So that you have — perhaps you are walking or sitting or doing whatever you are doing — you have an awareness of yourself extending above the limits of your body into a higher perspective. This is where the I AM presence dwells. It can be 12 to 30 feet or more above your head. Always with you. The contact, the connecting link between you and this presence is never broken. When you have had lifetimes caught up in the illusion of materialism, the cord has been thinner, and the I AM presence has been at a higher altitude from your bodies. In this lifetime, as you are working upon your ascension path, the I AM presence is much closer, drawing ever closer to you, and the channel of light is much wider and more vital. You see, it is the attention that you give to this aspect of yourself that feeds the connection.

You see, in your lives, you have experience of a certain amount of pain or a certain amount of separation. All of the difficulties that arise in physical life are as a result of the loss of contact, or the loss of the ability to experience fully, the presence of the I AM self. This is the source and the root of all illusion upon this Earth. It is the root of all darkness and divisiveness in human beings, and especially, of separation from all the blessings of life. You are intended to be able to experience your freedom, your sovereign power, and abilities to manifest. You are intended to be able to create much more readily, much more easily from the divine substance, whatever you require.

As a result of the darkness that has interpenetrated the illusion that the Earth beings have gotten caught up in, many other substitute situations have been set up, substitutions for that ability. Money was created and other sorts of structures to fill the need that was created by this separation. If you could create what you needed to eat out of the etheric substance of the God-presence, the light that surrounds you, you would not need to have a job in order to make money to buy bread.

So you are all volunteering to go back into that state wherein you are freed from this. This is the ascended state. Ultimately, you will not have these talents fully expressed until your ascension is completed. And yet, I tell you, that if you give yourself to your connection with the I AM presence, your ability to manifest, to create perfection in your lives — even in your material lives — will be enhanced greatly. So that in your lives — though you may still use money, and you may still use other sources of creativity to bring to yourself what you need — your creations can be much more miraculous. Many of you have already begun to experience some of this. It seems that what you need comes just at the perfect moment. You are receiving much training with regards to trust and faith, you see. And sometimes it does not come until the last minute.

But as you learn to trust and have faith in the I AM presence, in the Source, knowing that your source is not in the third dimension, you will be able to experience a more and more magical life even while you are waiting for your final ascension.

We have spoken in the past on self-mastery and manifestation. Your ability to control your manifestations, your thoughts, and your expressions, to express that which is of divine origin is very important now. For as you draw closer to your I AM presence and as your manifestation powers increase, all that you think and all that you project with your consciousness tends to manifest much more readily. So there is a responsibility inherent in this. A responsibility to attempt in every moment of your life to maintain a positive outlook: not to feed negativity, not to feed fear and doubts — to attempt to replace these with trust and faith.

And that brings me to another point I would like to make which is in alignment with what I have been discussing this evening, and that is "gratitude". Gratitude to your mighty I AM presence for all the blessings you have received: for all of the grace, for your awareness, for your dedication, even for the lessons you have learned, no matter how difficult they may have seemed sometimes. For gratitude is that which brings forth the presence of divine love into your life, into your body, and that gives you that love so you can share with others. So, having an "attitude of gratitude" acts as a great balm to soothe you through your trials and tribulations. Though you may have densities to clear, and obstacles in your lives, know that you are in the vast minority on this planet. Know that you are blessed beings. And there is no reason at all, ever, to feel sorry for yourselves. If you can see the picture with clarity, if you can gain a little bit of elevation, you will see how very blessed you are. And the time that remains for you, however long it may be before your ascension is attained, will be much more bearable, will be much more appreciated by you when you consider how many lifetimes, how many thousands of years you have existed here and how short the time really is before this miraculous transformation occurs for each of you. So, be grateful for this. Be grateful for all that you are receiving. When you feel sorry for yourself, try switching gears and feeling grateful for all that you have. When you feel that you are lacking, look at that which you have, and focus upon that, and call for your higher Self. Call for your teachers and guides to assist you in maintaining that focus, that positive focus. It is all-important at this time.

This energy of light and love that you feel in connecting with your higher Selves is to be loved, unconditionally. It is most appropriate to love the light for itself and not for that which the light can bring to you. It is not in alignment to meditate or to call upon your I AM presence because you desire to have a miraculous manifestation of some money or some other particular thing. This is not a perfect alignment. The perfect alignment is to focus upon that light because you love the light, and to connect with your I AM presence because you love it. If you can share the love that you feel for your I AM self, the response will be quite profound. It is always beneficial to call on your higher Self, your God-self, for assistance in any situation, but ultimately the purest reflection is simply to love the light for the light, because it feels so beautiful and because it is so wonderful in and of itself. Express it because it is that spontaneous, beautiful presence that you are, without regard for a return of any kind. The returns will come to you fast and furious if you can attain this state of purity. Another paradox on the path.

So, try to cultivate the love for your own I AM presence. You will cultivate it by feeling it. It is like a loved one that you have not seen for a long time. You feel love for that one, and yet, when you meet, the love is enhanced, the love is more profoundly expressed. And so it is with your own mighty I AM presence. When you feel in your meditations that contact, the love that you have within your beings is expressed. It surrounds you, it comes through. It is felt. It is felt as devotion, the experience of devotion — the love for the God-presence, the longing for the God-presence. So you could say that you can have a love affair within yourself that is quite extraordinary, that brings you an incredible amount of divine love and ecstasy.

So, let us do a little meditation together, and we will perhaps experience more of this presence that I have been referring to this evening. This is not something that is difficult. It is something that occurs quite spontaneously, when you totally relax yourself. You see, you can't escape from yourself, no matter how hard you try. So if you stop trying to escape from yourself, your Self will find you. And it will bestow upon you a great blessing of divine love. It is simply a matter of attaining that stillness within — that stillness wherein your I AM presence can find you and connect with you. It is always chasing you, and it chases you until you stop running and still yourself enough for it to catch up with you.

So, relax and breathe. Let your bodies be relaxed. As you breathe you may feel an awareness of the light within, your higher chakras, your third eye and your crown. If you feel a light within your heads, you may simply experience it. Try to maintain your focused, relaxed breathing. We are surrounding this room with a beautiful light. You are insulated and protected. You are safe and secure. Dense energies from the external world cannot penetrate.

Now I will teach you a very effective affirmation to use that will dramatically enhance your contact with your I AM presence. It is very simple, I am sure you have heard it before: "I AM THAT I AM."

Repeat this internally, several times, to yourselves, as you breathe. In affirming this, you are calling forth and acknowledging your oneness with the mighty I AM presence, with your God-self. "I AM THAT I AM" affirms that you and your I AM presence are one.

So we will have some silence now. I would like to ask that if you are feeling any sensations, simply relax and breathe and focus. You may feel your I AM presence above you, coming down around you. You may feel certain sensations over your heads or your meditation may be enhanced, whatever you feel. I ask you each — individually, silently — to affirm one more time, and then we will be in silence for a few minutes.

So, my bright ones, I thank you for your undivided attention this evening. I thank you for choosing St. Germain over the Monday night football game! Very discriminating of you to do so! I trust that the work that we have done this evening will be of great benefit to you. It is a time of great excitement, as I have said, great enthusiasm on our parts — and great joy. For the divine love is truly all encompassing: it surrounds the planet, it surrounds each individual soul with many blessings. And blessed are you who have the capacity to open to receive these blessings, and to align yourself with them rather than resisting. Resistance to this divine love creates confusion. Acceptance of this divine love creates joy and peace and many wonderful experiences.

So thank you, my friends. As always, it has been a great pleasure to address you. You are all doing wonderfully. Good night.

Aligning with Your Earth Mission

ARCHANGEL MICHAEL

Good Evening and welcome. This is Archangel Michael. Having solved the first mystery of the evening, I will go on to greater and deeper mysteries. We must identify ourselves right from the start, or you will spend half of the channeling trying to figure out who it is! It's such a peaceful night; everyone is so quiet, so receptive. You know, you are all getting to be quite expanded and quite beautiful to view. You may feel that you are the same as you have always been, but you have evolved a great deal. The evidence is not existent in the physical plane as much as it is upon the spiritual planes. Your physical bodies have not changed as much as your spiritual bodies have. You are larger and brighter I would say. So congratulations to you. It has been a very interesting journey, has it not? And yet, all the ground that we have covered so far is but the beginning. It is but the foundation for the wonderful building that we will construct together. It is the foundation for your Earth missions, the completion of which is imminent, as you know. And this is what I would like to speak with you about this evening.

I would like to give you my viewpoint, my perspective, concerning what you refer to as your Earth missions. This is a very interesting subject for most of you. You have all asked yourselves, from time to time, what your Earth mission is, what you are doing here, what you are supposed to be accomplishing? Being the sincere aspirants that you are, you all have a sincere desire to get on with it, to get on to the completion. Some of you want to get on with it so that you can get off the planet! Some of you just want to get on with it regardless of where that takes you. I think the discussion we will have tonight will be one of several, perhaps, to address this subject, for it is very important. So know that what I tell you this evening is from my perspective. There are others who may wish to share their perspectives on this subject in other gatherings.

There is within each human being, especially those who are evolving upon the spiritual path, a strong desire for completion, a strong desire for alignment with their individual Earth missions. And your Earth missions involve, you might say, the service projects that you are engaged in here in third-dimensional reality. And by project, I do not mean simply some external activity limited to this lifetime, but I would say your Earth missions are very all-inclusive, and encompass all of your Earth incarnations. And you have many layers within your overall missions. You have your primary directive, which is identical to that of every other evolving being. This is a unifying factor. Your mission at this level, of course, is to evolve towards greater awareness, higher realization, and to grow within the universal hierarchy closer and closer to Source, serving the Creator's divine plan. As you proceed upon this extended journey you are capable of absorbing, and sharing, and experiencing more of that essential life force. You expand and open and contain much more. Just as in your Earth lives, say some years ago, before you were involved in your spiritual path, you had your ideas, your conceptions, your life. And now, as you look back upon it, you can see how much more love and light you contain, how much closer you feel to the Source. So even within this tiny perspective you can get an idea of the overall mission of the soul of an evolving being. This is your primary directive. This is the foundation upon which all other activities are founded.

Within this context, if you take it to another level, you could say that your mission, let me say the service project that you are engaged in, involves being so called "Starseeds." You chose to come to this world many thousands of years ago from higher dimensions, for the evolvement of yourselves and the human species, all leading to this wonderful lifetime that we are sharing at this time. Isn't it amazing how many lifetimes you have waited for this! And now you are here, you have made it, you have succeeded. So again, congratulations are in order. And if you are perhaps feeling that you have not succeeded, or that you have not evolved to the degree that you desire, I suggest you lay that thought aside and simply look at what you have attained in all of these lifetimes. Look at how open and prepared you are to return to the higher dimensions from which you came. That is quite an accomplishment: to fall asleep, to reawaken, to fall asleep many times and to reawaken many times. The veils will be removed very soon.

So within the context of your prime directive, you have accepted this other mission, this service project you have taken on. You'll notice we have not gotten down to any personal projects, or anything relating to this particular lifetime yet. And this second layer of your mission also involves a unification of sorts. You are connected with all the other Starseeds, all the volunteers who took on this same project as a group effort. And this is another layer of your mission. And within all of this are your unique personalities and talents, the individual skills and experiences you have brought to bear on this Earth mission. You have carried these talents throughout your lifetimes, and manifested in many different ways, ideally all of them reflecting the Divine. So you came to this particular lifetime open and prepared for your next step — waiting to complete your service, your mission — gathering information and intuitional evidence along the way based upon your own experiences and understandings about what that could mean to you. You have all been going through your various processes about it, trying to understand what is an Earth mission after all. And now you find yourselves here, involved with the ascension. It is at this point that your Earth mission is truly coming into focus, you see. For as these higher-dimensional energies flood you each day, each night, they are reawakening you to the higher Self, and to your unique individual talents and gifts. And this is moving you to this next level of the mission, that which is particular to you in this lifetime, in this particular moment in history. This is the area on which I would like to focus my discussion this evening.

First of all, I think it is important to note that your mission is, most of all, tied in with the first and second directives I have already spoken about. Your mission is not necessarily one particular activity, one particular service project, in this third-dimensional reality. That is, you did not come here to become a great auto mechanic, though this may be something that you accomplish. You did not come here to establish a world-wide computer network, though this may be something that you work on. Your mission is, and always has been, to be one hundred percent available to the guidance of your higher Self and of Source, to make yourselves available to that in each moment.

It is oftentimes a point of confusion with human beings, feeling that they have found their particular Earth mission, when what they have found is an activity that feels like service to them at a particular time. And they can confuse that activity with their Earth mission. You could say, "Oh I am here to become a channel, and to channel this ascended master information. This is my Earth mission." But this is an activity, it is not the Earth mission. It is a manifestation of that. For in the next week or the next month or year the tables could turn, and that being who was thinking they were here to be a channel exclusively may find themselves for some mysterious reason unable to channel any longer, or having lost interest in that particular activity. So has that person failed in their mission? Not at all. Your mission is to follow Spirit in each moment, wherever that guidance leads. So in one sense I would say most of you are accomplishing your missions quite beautifully, even those who may feel that you do not have any idea what your Earth mission might be. If you are relating to the mission as an activity, you may have a time to wait while you clear that confusion. The way that you connect with the experience of fulfilling your Earth mission is, of course, to follow your joy, follow your heart, follow your guidance. Open yourselves in meditation and channeling, and spontaneously follow your spirit where it leads you. This is the proper attitude for one who is wishing to align with their Earth mission. It is not something that you do, it is something that you become. Does that make it simpler?

Others have come through and discussed service with you, and I believe I have stated the fact that service is not an activity; it is an experience of action connected with the consciousness of the Divine. It has nothing to do with a particular activity, for no activity is inherently any more a service than any other. Now there may come a time, after you have applied yourself with sincerity and devotion to your path, that you will be granted service opportunities. You will be granted service projects within this lifetime, and this can be a very exciting experience for you. It is also, at times, a very confronting experience. It tends to push your buttons, to bring out your fears and feelings of inadequacy, this sort of thing. It also activates a great deal of grace in your lives. In fact, I would say if you are having the experience of more presence — of spiritual masters around you and in your homes — and if you are having the feeling perhaps of skating out on thin ice, of not really knowing what you're doing, but following your hearts, I would say that you are being prepared for service. There is an aspect of the mission that tends to be something that stretches you a little bit, or demands greater devotion, surrender, and trust. It may seem much easier to remain in your old patterns of existence. But you will not be able to fit your fifth-dimensional consciousness into these old limited patterns. You will find that you are having to expand a little bit, in order to perform activities that are more of a healing and serving nature.

It comes with the territory you see, that feeling of being a little bit beyond your limits, of not really knowing what you are going to do a little bit down the road, but knowing what you feel inside of yourself in the moment and doing that. It is like walking out on a limb, not knowing for sure that the limb will support you, but trusting. And you all do this in many ways in your lives each day. So to fulfill your mission does not mean that you need to become as Jesus was, make a spectacle of your life and create a lot of commotion. It is as simple as following your intuition, following your guidance, acting out of faith rather than fear. It's a journey, and its meaning and direction can only be experienced from moment to moment. Oftentimes an aspect of this journey is that you are only given information enough to take you to the next step, the next level, the next stage. You are not generally given information concerning your entire lifetime and all the activities you will perform. This would be too much. In fact, Spirit is much more spontaneous than that. So any of you who feel you have a destiny that is carved in stone for this lifetime, I would seriously reconsider that notion.

Spirit will use any being that is open in the most appropriate way in any situation at any time. In fact, many beings who were intended or had capacities to do activities such as teaching or channeling, to do many wonderful acts of service, have remained in the sleep state. And others are finding their way to the forefront. Substitutions are being made, and some are offered opportunities that another may have bypassed through their reticence. So you see, the Creator and His servants, the Angelic Hosts and the ascended masters, are using whatever means are at their disposal to accomplish their mission. And you are some of the means that are at our disposal on the Earth plane at this time. The more you can open yourselves, the more you can be utilized, the more you can experience of service.

So again, there are beings who have an overblown sense of mission, and there are others who have an under-developed sense of mission. Really, it is the middle ground that we are after here. Some beings are feeling that they are vitally important to the saving of the planet, that they are mighty servants of God. I would recommend that this is not the correct attitude. This can result from an ego identification with a particular service project, or a particular spiritual gift or talent. Then there are others, and I think most of you would fall into this category, who tend to be a little bit more on the meek side, having an under-developed sense of your own magnificence. This is your humility, but also your fear. For those who are in this category, I would say it is simply a matter of following your joy and opening yourself, of making a little space in your consciousness for something new to enter. It could be a new gift, a new talent, a new connection with another human being. It could be a smile. It could be any number of experiences.

There will come those times when you have opportunities and choices to make as to whether you are going to accept a new experience or not. You have all had this experience, so I know you are aware of what I am speaking of. Perhaps you have criticized yourselves for apparent failures in opening to new things, for giving in to fear, etc. Well, you can erase those thoughts from your mind, because that's how you learn. You see, you learn through what feels good to you. And more and more it feels good to open and to go beyond, to take the next step into the next stage. And it feels less good to stay back in old patterns. You see, you are following your joy again. And it is a step by step unfoldment for each of you. So I would say, in defining your Earth missions at this time, that it is the step by step unfolding of your own divinity, and whatever action occurs spontaneously out of that unfoldment is in alignment with your Earth mission.

So your mission involves that which you enjoy, and also that which may create some fear within you, because it is pushing you beyond your limits a little bit. It is that which you surrender to — the next step in your growth — knowing if you remain at the previous step you will not feel so excited by life, you will feel a little more sleepy and not so much in joy. And your appetite for joy grows with each step. You are given new steps, new opportunities. And by taking one step at a time, one moment at a time, I think each of you in this room have the potential to find yourselves doing wonderful activities of service, wonderful manifestations of love and healing. Simply by taking one moment at a time, one breath at a time and one step at a time to follow your joy, to be a little bit courageous in opening to the new, you will manifest many wonders.

There is a great need for love on this planet, and a great need for those who have the ability to radiate that. This is the highest service that you can perform at this time. It can manifest in many ways, yet it always feels like love. It can manifest in a channeling or in a healing, or it can manifest in a telephone conversation. It can manifest in any number of ways, in relationship. The relationship between Source and humanity requires a bridge. It sometimes requires a human body that is in alignment with the Divine to approach another human that is still sleeping, to make that connection. Those beings who are unable to awaken at this time are not able to experience the presence of their higher Selves, the presence of the ascended masters, or the Angelic Host, who are here.

We are here as you know. Many of you have been overwhelmed by our presence lately. We are here with great power, and yet even with all of this light and love, it still seems to require, for many, a human factor. And this is where the Starseeds come into play: having physical bodies, having an understanding through all of your lifetimes of experience, knowing how to relate to beings who are still asleep, though longing in their hearts to awaken and to feel the joy. So, generally speaking, your Earth missions will somehow assist in the process of connecting human beings with their Divine Source, activating and healing, and all of this with love. It can be quite simple, or it can be quite involved, but the end results are the same.

So, we need some beings who are willing to celebrate — celebrate in the face of apparent chaos, in the face of density, and not give into fear. To continually shine that light and love as beacons and examples. And everyone who is in this room, and everyone who will hear these words in the future, has within them the capacity to be one who has fully aligned with the Earth mission. So I encourage you my friends. I encourage you to follow your enjoyment. When you have a choice between something new and exciting and something old and stale, why not try something new and exciting? You never know where it's going to lead you. This is how all of the great masters who have walked the Earth began.

There was once a great master who, as a child, walked by someone delivering a spiritual discourse under a tree. Perhaps it was an old man with a beard, but for some reason the boy stopped to listen. He knew he was going to be late for school, but something in his heart made him choose to stop for a minute to listen to the words of spiritual discourse rather than going along in his usual way . And that moment awakened something in that individual being, and he was inspired to study and to meditate, and one day became a great Avatar. All because he stopped that one moment and followed his joy.

Your moments are no different. Sometimes it might be choosing to sit and meditate when you feel the presence of one of your guides in the middle of your day. I think you have all had that experience, where you are busily occupying yourselves with some project or some work, and you stop for a second and feel a presence surrounding you. You know that at that moment if you were to stop and breathe you would perhaps have a little window of opportunity to take you into a higher realm of consciousness, or to receive some guidance. And in that moment you have the opportunity to choose either to continue in your patterned behavior, or to stop for a second and explore.

You see, it is very simple. Perhaps if you had stopped you would have heard a message that was of incredible importance. Perhaps you would have had an experience that led you, gave you an idea or inspiration for something entirely new in your life. Something that brought joy, prosperity, abundance. Perhaps it was a message that directed you to meet someone who connected with you in a wonderful relationship. All because you stopped for that moment and followed your joy. This is what I am speaking of. I am not speaking of standing in front of the United Nations and bringing the house down. One day there will be time for that, perhaps.

Spirit will guide you on your way in small steps, with the perfect steps for you. And if you attend to the small steps you will never have to take a large step, because you will already be there, one small step away from whatever that goal is for you. And remember, your goal is not to become the best auto mechanic or the best computer systems networker or any of those things. Your goal is to unfold the incredible bliss and grace and love. It is so profound, it is so overwhelming, that it is necessary to take you gradually into that experience. If it were to manifest in all its implications in one moment you would not be able to survive it. That is how much love there is for you, that is how much light, how much bliss there is for you. So your Earth missions, your service opportunities, while they are for the benefit of humanity and the sharing of the light, they are also profoundly for yourselves. For you contracted to be here in this world to have service opportunities galore. You knew that these service opportunities would lead you into advanced states. I think many of you thought this mission looked like a good short cut. "I think I'll accept this service opportunity, this project to incarnate on the Earth in third-dimensional reality. I'm ready to go. If I do this I will receive incredible opportunities for advancement. I will experience even more bliss." And then, after your Earth incarnation, perhaps you were feeling simply, "How am I going to survive this in the first place?" It was a little more intense than you bargained for, perhaps. But know that only those beings who were considered fully capable were accepted. Many volunteers were refused.

So, in unfolding yourselves, you will realize just how powerful you are. And in the days to come, after the ascension has occurred, when you find yourselves back in more familiar territory, you will all look at one another and you will have shared something truly incredible. And you will have benefited. You will be having opportunities for expansion just as you had planned. So it is time for you to detach a little from the survival mode and open to your divine mode of operation. Open to that part of you that knows why you are here. That will assist you in getting down to the particulars about your own lives, how you fit into the program, and how you can maximize these days that are remaining to you. And these days are few. After all of your lifetimes, it is as the wink of an eye that is remaining in your Earth experience, in your limited third-dimensional experience at least.

So even this experience that you are sometimes cursing and longing to be rid of is an opportunity for you. It is an opportunity that may not come again. Next time others will be chosen. That's the way of the universal evolvement. So take advantage of your situations and follow your joy. See where it leads you. You will not be disappointed. Love yourselves and avoid self-criticism. There is no one to compare yourself against. There is only following your particular joy and opening, surrendering, detaching, and allowing — one small step after another into the completion of your Earth mission.

So, I think it's meditation time again. You've noticed we have a pattern these days in our classes: after the discourse comes the meditation. When we think of a better way to do it, we will change things. This seems to be working rather effectively, as every time we meet I see you glowing so much more brightly. We must be doing something right! So tonight I will assist you in your meditation. If you would like I will assist in severing your attachments. We will raise you to a little bit higher level in meditation so as to stretch those cords so I can get at them. It is beneficial in the accomplishment of your Earth missions to be detached from past limitations, past beliefs, all sorts of limiting factors. As you climb on your path, you will feel a pulling at you from behind, calling for you to turn back. And at that point it is very beneficial for you to call upon my presence. I will cut the cords and allow you to spring forward. So let's just meditate a little bit together on our breathing and enjoy.

Well done, my friends, well done indeed! So much is occurring invisibly. Before I take my leave I would like to bring up one more point, something to help to make it easier for you, you who are striving to attain perfection. I ask you to open to an attitude adjustment. Perhaps you could view your mission as something that you relax into. Relax into your own divine power and presence. Trust it, and it will guide you to completion, to the completion of your Earth sojourn. So until we meet again, good night.

Eleven

Spiral of Light

Mother Mary

Good evening, dear ones. It is a pleasure to be with you. This is Mother Mary, here in my male disguise. Don't let these looks deceive you, it is I. I greet you with love this evening. And we have much to share, as much as we can manage to bring through. Know that each of you, if you are willing, will be utilized as channels this evening — of my presence, Lord Sananda's presence, and of all the masters that are here gathered. Let's make it a group endeavor, shall we? Relax yourselves and breathe with me. I ask that you be natural. Pretend that you are sitting in your own living room. My energies this evening will be most healing to you. And you may feel the need for this, as it has been a rather intense week of purification here on planet Earth and within your very bodies. So, if you will open yourselves to receive with sincerity and trust, you shall receive — through the channel of your own hearts — beautiful healing energies this evening.

Such a light now shines. Such a love, through and upon this planet, through and upon you as beings of this world, and you are feeling this. It is awakening you, inspiring you to these strange gatherings, this strange company. And when you arrive you realize your brothers and sisters are here waiting for you. For we truly are gathering the family of Light Workers on a garland of love and light that is the essence, that is the source, purpose, and meaning of your existence. Though each of you are a unique flower on the garland, that which binds all together is that essence of love and light. It is a time for unification, acceptance, and love, for yourselves and for all. It is a time to release that which you have held in your minds and egos of judgment and criticism, of spiritual ego.

You see, there is no time for this any longer. It is a time for unity and love, a time to be once again as children, aligned with the Spirit within you and acting from Spirit in each moment of your lives. It is time to release from your consciousness and from your lives those extraneous belief systems, patterns, habits, which no longer serve the unification and enlightenment process. Rather, it is time to go into the essence of what you are, and discover the meaning of life beyond those thought forms and patterns of belief you have been programmed to believe are reality. All that you require exists within you, waiting for you to tune in to the power and majesty that awaits. It is your divine responsibility now to accept the challenge that is before you.

There are those in this world who would look at people who sit and meditate each day as escapists; "Oh look, they are having difficulty dealing with reality so they are trying to escape." Well, if you have difficulty dealing with the reality of this world, it is merely a sign that you are not insane! For indeed, what has been programmed into you as reality in this world is truly but a twisted shadow of reality as it truly exists in higher dimensions, in worlds that are aligned with the divine plan. The alignment and purification of this world are well under way. The energies that have opened your hearts, that have brought you to this gathering, that have allowed you to release fear, that have inspired you — these energies purify this planet and purify you. They align you with the true meaning and true reality of life.

Perhaps you have been feeling within yourselves an increased inspiration to return to the experience of love and peace, to return to Source, to once again feel the presence of that Creator being that exists within each of you. Truly the energies of this activation period upon planet Earth are awakening you to this. Sometimes you're not even sure why you are doing what you're doing. It feels almost as if your higher Self is taking control of your life. It is! You can put up a good fight, or you can surrender. You see, you have a previous commitment, a knowingness, that has kept you from honoring all the many commitments that you've learned from your parents and teachers and social systems. What is it that has made you look beyond to the real meaning? It is a prior commitment that is existing in your hearts, in your souls, in your beings, to awaken at this time and to share in the wonderful birthing process of the planet, the re-birthing of a planet into the higher dimensions. You are here, my dear ones, not as bystanders or mere spectators, but as active participants. The call goes out to you to accept the challenge of your divinity, to release separatism and ego, to surrender the reins of your life to Spirit, your higher Self, that part of you which truly knows what's going on, and what you are meant to do. And how glorious your victory will be, your victory over death and fear and limitation.

You have all experienced, in your lives, being purposeful. In fact, just about everything that you do in your lives is for a certain purpose. You go to your jobs to make money so that you can pay your rent or your mortgage, etc. You go to the store to buy food so that you can maintain your physical body and not get in trouble with your spouse! Everything that you do, you do with purpose. If a being on this planet exists in a state of purposelessness, they are labeled emotionally disturbed or insane. They just wander the streets all day. Their lives seem to have no purpose. You are beings constructed and created with purpose, and yet within all of those purposes that you fulfill each day to maintain your life, there is a divine purpose underlying all of this. There is a meaning behind the activities that you undertake to sustain your life here on this world. Some of you are very organized. Some of you are more scattered in your ways and means of doing business here on the planet Earth. But there is a meaning and a purpose you are here to uncover, beyond the cycles of activity you perform just to maintain your physical and emotional lives. It is enlightenment. It is realization. It is ascension. It is a growth into another level of awareness.

There are two spirals in effect now on this world, in this universe. There is an upwardly moving spiral of light, that leads to the Divine Source — and those who surrender to Spirit are walking this wonderful spiral, are experiencing an upliftment. And there is a spiral of downward motion, of contraction and fear. And those who are resisting Spirit are experiencing this.

At this time you have a choice to make. And in making your choice, you will be given other choices about what you wish to include in your life, what you wish to experience or let go of. I suggest you let go of those downwardly spiraling energies and open to receive that which is so bountifully flowing now. You are living through a time that has not occurred before on this planet, and each of you will witness incredible wonders and transformations. Your hearts are aware now that it is no longer "business as usual" for you or for this world, and yet you receive through your social programming and your media all the signs and signals that things are just as they always were. So there is a choice for you. What will you believe — your own heart, which is calling for that reunion with your Creator, or those external sources which tell you you had better plan for your retirement, work hard, don't step out of line, don't do anything that will attract attention to yourself, and maybe the world will leave you alone? I am sure that some of you are at odds at times as to which pattern or reality you choose to believe. And yet you shall witness in this lifetime the unfoldment of the divine plan for this world, which is but a part of the divine plan as it unfolds for all worlds and all universes.

It is the end of a cycle, a great cosmic cycle. This is why your hearts are opening, your spiritual faculties are opening and awakening. This is why you have evenings of channelings occurring in living rooms, where at one time you might have had a "beer blast!" We will have another kind of blast this evening: a light blast. So awaken to the meaning of this life now. Take these words as another indication. Take these energies of love and light into your being. Breathe with me. Feel the truth, the essence. Your bodies are being transformed. You are becoming lighter. That which is dense within your emotions, your physical bodies, your mental bodies, is being purified and released as you rise in consciousness and actually raise the vibrational frequency of your molecules and cells.

This is what you have been waiting for: liberation from the mundane, liberation into truth and essence and light. What I refer to as truth is not anything that we can speak of in language. You have heard the phrase perhaps in your lives — when someone gains an understanding of a certain principle, they say, "Oh, now I see the light." That's not what we're talking about at all. We are talking about light itself: the light that you are, the light that can not be put into language, the light which radiates through you now, which awakens and opens the chakra of your third eye, that fills you with the brilliant God-presence. Then you will see the light! Quite a bit different isn't it, for those of you who know what I am speaking of.

There are many putting forth reality pictures at this time that can sound very terrifying and calamitous. There are those who truly feel this is the end of the world and we had better repent, that we are all going to reap our just desserts, and this frightens them. For those who feel unworthy or who feel guilt at having done some imagined crimes or other, it must be a very terrifying reality perspective to believe in. Yet we tell you that it is a time of generosity and grace and blessings. A time of harvest for those souls who truly desire to be one with Spirit, and to go beyond the limited cycle of birth and death that you have experienced. How many lifetimes has it taken you to get to this moment? Where did you come from before you had your lifetimes here on planet Earth? Who are you, aside from this physical body that goes to the grocery store? What is the purpose of having come to this planet and taken lifetime after lifetime, physical embodiment after physical embodiment? I don't think it was to become a millionaire. Many of you have been millionaires. You died anyway! You had a nice expensive casket. Maybe bones from your previous incarnations are still keeping very well. Maybe in that lifetime you realized there must be something more than the endless gathering of wealth, the endless gathering of anything. And truly there is. And truly, now is the time that you shall reap the rewards of your evolution.

It is a matter of going within, into the stillness that exists within you, into the Light that exists within you. This is where you will witness and know truth. Not through these words. Not through any scriptures. Not through any teachings. The purpose of teachings is to point the finger of guidance back to you, and not to your mind or your ego personality, but to your heart, your being, your essence. And the purpose of teachings of any kind, if they are pure teachings, is to empower you toward God-realization, to help you to go within to witness your own divinity, to become one with the Christ, and to fulfill the purposes that you came here to fulfill. Realize your oneness with the Creator. Attain the ascension, which will liberate you once and for always from the rounds of birth and death. All this is available to you in this lifetime. How fortunate you must be, how wise you must be to have chosen to be alive at this time.

So my beloved ones, there is so much love that pours forth to you now. It is our heart's desire that you open your hearts and feel this. It is a two way street. You must open and learn to receive divine love. It does not come from external sources, but through the channel of your higher Self, through your open heart, to fill you with bliss and purpose. It is within you. The kingdom of heaven is within you. And in all likelihood this is your last lifetime on planet Earth. So I would suggest it is a good one to get it right! There is more than adequate grace and blessings now to make it easier than ever to go within, to experience who you are. Meditation practice is something you can all experience. It does you little good to think that you are a master if you are not manifesting as a master, if you are not feeling and being and radiating that light and love. Now is the time for those of you who truly desire to go beyond ideas of enlightenment, into the light itself, into your light bodies. And as your body is transformed into light, you will join with the ascended masters who await you in the higher dimensions. We are calling you to join us.

So the meaning and purpose of this life, from my perspective, is enlightenment. And everything that you do in your physical lives and your emotional lives is intended to be in support of your enlightenment. You eat food so that you will have the physical strength to maintain your body form, so that you can experience the light and love and service of the Creator. You earn money so that you can have a roof over your heads, so you have a place to meditate without freezing. It's all very simple from our standpoint. I think you will find, if you truly give yourself to Spirit, that it will become very simple for you also. You will know what is extraneous and what desires do not serve you. And that desire which does serve you will be amplified, the desire that exists in your heart to return to Source, to unfold your Earth missions.

To be a Light Worker — one intended to awaken and become a master at this time — who is still attempting to live a limited third-dimensional existence, can be a very painful affair. For the entire power of the universe and the Creator is blossoming forth within you, calling you to open and arise. If you have felt resistance in your bodies to spiritual growth, it is only the part of you which clings to that limited security of the ego. There is a point at which the ego is surrendered to the higher Self. It is purified, given back to you to be used in a very wonderful way in service in this world, and so you can still go to the grocery store.

You know there are many enlightened beings shopping at grocery stores this very moment! They haven't escaped from the world at all. In fact, they are more present than ever, more abundant and prosperous than ever, more in love than ever, because they have surrendered their egos to Spirit, to the divine car wash, and all that was gritty and grimy and blocking the flow of grace has been removed. Just as you will receive purified egos, you will receive purified physical bodies of light in the ascension experience. Anyone care for a trade-in? Aren't your vehicles showing their mileage a little bit? I think someone turned back the odometer on this one!

There is so much love for you my dear ones, so much assistance. I ask you to go within. In your daily lives, consistently give yourselves to meditation practice. If you don't know how to meditate, I will teach you a very simple and profound technique to use. There may be one or two of you who are still not meditating. There may be twenty or thirty of you — this is not mine to judge. Just breathe in silence with your eyes closed. Call upon guidance, Lord Sananda — call upon all of your teachers and guides to be with you, and ask that you be aligned with your spirit and feel the presence of your divinity. Just breathe and let go of your thoughts, and let your Creator, your higher Self, fill you with love and light. Focus in this way on your breathing. Go beyond the mind, go into the stillness. Sounds too simple, doesn't it? Do you know that every avatar and master has revealed this technique, and Lord Sananda did reveal this technique to his initiates. Your breath is the link, your connection with Source. It is that which opens the channel within you to your divinity and brings the light into your body. You've got to bring the light into your body. You've got to get to know the light. Live with it, merge with it. Let the light guide you. Let it open your chakras and cement the contact with your higher Self so that you can receive messages and guidance, so you don't feel alone, so you feel no separation.

The illusion of separation is what keeps you feeling limited — the belief in separation. You are not separate from your Creator. You are one with your Creator. You happen to have accepted the belief system that you are separate, that you needed to work your way back through good actions, religious activities or spiritual practices. So in your meditation practice, perhaps you could attempt to release that subconscious belief in separation. Affirm that you are one, and then meditate to enjoy that expression of oneness, rather than to try to re-create it. It already exists.

So, it has been an honor to be with you, my dear ones. Call upon me for healing, for nurturing. I love you so much. Go within. Give yourself to Spirit. Now is the time. Now is the time you have awaited. Take advantage of it. So, I ask your kind permission to meditate with me in silence for a few moments, as I share a final blessing. Good night.

ABOUT THE AUTHOR ❧❧❧

Eric Klein

Eric Klein was initiated and began his spiritual path of meditation and service in 1972. He began conscious channeling of the masters in 1986 and evolved into a period of inner instruction from many ascended teachers. The first public channelings began in 1988 with weekly evening gatherings, which then evolved into more specific classes and workshops under guidance from Sananda.

Eric and his wife, Christine, continue to live in Santa Cruz, California. Christine is an acupuncturist and also a channel. Together, they have traveled extensively across the United States, channeling and teaching workshops in support of the personal and planetary ascension process. They continue to channel the masters to include Sananda, Ashtar, Archangel Michael, St. Germain, Kuan Yin, Kuthumi, El Morya, Mother Mary, Serapis Bey, Hilarion, and others.

Readings Suggested by the Author ❖❖❖

An Ascension Handbook by Tony Stubbs, Oughten House Publications (available at New Age bookstores)

On Eagle's Wings by Ariana Sheran, Cloverleaf Connection (available through Oughten House Publications)

Bridge Into Light by Fred and Pam Cameron, Oughten House Publications, (available at New Age bookstores)

On Earth Assignment, Project: Earth Evacuation, and *Ashtar, A Tribute* by Tuella. Guardian Action International, PO Box 27725, Salt Lake City, UT 84127

Conclave: Meetings of the Ones, Vols. I, II, III and *IV* by Tuieta. Portals of Light, PO Box 15621, Ft. Wayne, IN 46885

E. T. 101 The Cosmic Instruction Manual by Diana Luppi. Intergalactic Council Publications (available through Oughten House Publications)

Unveiled Mysteries and the Magic Presence by Godfrey Ray King, St. Germain Press (available at New Age bookstores)

The Keys of Enoch by J. J. Hurtak, Academy of Future Science (available at New Age bookstores)

The Urantia Book by The Urantia Foundation (available at New Age bookstores)

Serapis Bey: Dossier On the Ascension by Mark Prophet, Summit University Press

ABOUT THE PUBLISHER AND LOGO ᴥ

The name "Oughten" was revealed to the publisher thirteen years ago after three weeks of meditation and contemplation. The combined effect of each letter connotes the theme of humanity's ascension on a planetary level.

The logo represents a new world rising from its former condition. The planet ascends from the darker to the lighter. Our knowledge of a dark and mysterious universe becomes transmuted by our rising planet's consciousness — glorious and spiritual. The grace of God transmutes the past into gold as we ascend beyond it and into the millennium.

ABOUT THE ARTIST ᴥᴥᴥ

Reverend Cathie Beach is a clairvoyant healer who lives in Santa Cruz, California. Besides illustrating book covers, she creates personalized, healing drawings. The images may be symbolic or abstract, and the colors resonate with an individual's energy system, giving support and balance. Many people are now using these drawings for gentle healing and personal empowerment. For additional information, please contact Oughten House.

PUBLISHER'S COMMENT ✧✧✧

Our mission and purpose is to publish ascension books and complementary material for all peoples and all children worldwide.

We currently serve over twenty authors who have books, manuscripts, and numerous tapes in production. Most of our authors channel Sananda, Ashtar, Archangel Michael, St. Germain, Archangel Ariel, Hilarion, Mother Mary, and Kwan Yin. They need your support to get their channeled messages to all nations. Oughten House Publications welcomes your interest and petitions your overall support and association in this momentous and timely endeavor.

We urge you to share the information with your friends, join our network and high-spirit affiliations. Our financial proceeds are recycled into producing new ascension books and expanding our distribution worldwide. If you have the means to contribute or invest in this process, then please contact us.

OUGHTEN HOUSE PUBLICATIONS ❧❧

Our imprint includes books in a variety of fields and disciplines which emphasize the rising planetary consciousness. Literature which relates to the ascension process is our primary line. We are also cultivating a line of thoughtful and beautifully illustrated children's books, which deal with spirituality, angels, mystical realms, and God, the Creator. Our third line of books deals with societal matters, personal growth, poetry, and publications on extraterrestrials.

The Crystal Stair: A Guide to the Ascension, by Eric Klein
ISBN 1-880666-06-5, $12.95

An Ascension Handbook A practical, in-depth, how-to manual on the ascension process, by Tony Stubbs
ISBN1-880666-08-1, $11.95

Shar Dea: Empress of Peace A novel about an ascended master's return to the planet, by Robert V. Gerard
ISBN 0-916383-40-7, $8.95

Bridge Into Light: Your Connection to Spiritual Guidance A how-to book on meditating and channeling, by Pam and Fred Cameron — ISBN 1-880666-07-3, $11.95

The Inner Door: Channeled Discourses from the Ascended Masters on Self-Mastery and Ascension, by Eric Klein
Volume One: ISBN 1-880666-03-0, $14.50
Volume Two: ISBN 1-880666-16-2, $14.50

Japanese Brushwork Inspirational Cards Created by Andrew Bonnici and printed in earth-tone colors. Cards reflect Zen meditations or metaphors of wisdom with beautiful Japanese brushwork and calligraphy. Two sets available, six cards each, at $14.50 per set

Ascension Tapes A series of channeled and meditation tapes on the ascension process, by Eric and Christine Klein (available through Oughten House Publications)

Nature Walk Introducing "Pelfius," the lively little Nature Spirit who lives among the trees, the rivers, and the stars. For children from 2 years and up (adults too!). A beautifully illustrated booklet, by Susan Hays Meredith ISBN 1-880666-09-X, $4.95

Synergic Power: Beyond Domination, Beyond Permissiveness This book examins the concept of power and how to use power *with* people, not over or against them; by James H. and Margureite Craig, ISBN 0-914158-28-7, $8.95

Power From Within A workbook to assist women in discovering their power and expressing it in creative, caring ways. Learn how to center and channel your energies of mind, body, and spirit. This is an excellent self-paced workbook, by Margureite Craig, Sheila Merle Johnson, and Mary Lautner, ISBN 0-914158-27-9, $5.00

Partial Listing of Forthcoming Books

An Ascension Journal Write your own ascension story by utilizing the techniques offered in the introductory pages of this journal, by Nicole Christine ISBN 1-880666-18-9, $11.95

Handling Verbal Confrontations: Take the FEAR Out of Facing Others Gain peace of mind through accurate communication; learn the art of peaceful confrontation, by Rob Gerard — ISBN 1-880666-05-7, $14.95

The Corporate Mule Spirituality in the organization exists! A fast-paced comedy, by Rob Gerard
ISBN 1-880666-04-9, $9.95

Yes, Yes One Can: A Spiritual Guide to Upcoming Earth Changes Extraterrestrials offer us warnings and messages of love, by Christine Wong
ISBN 1-880666-13-8, $7.95

The Extraterrestrial Vision The entity Theodore presents a summary of extraterrestrial involvement with Earth: past, present, and future. Channeled by Gina Lake

The Violet Fire A story of a family's journey toward ascension, by Faith Summer

Spaceships Overhead Channelings accompanied by photographs produced by extraterrestrials. Channeled by Christine Wong

Seven Steps to Joy: In a Changing World This workbook shows how to access advanced Intelligence, by Prem Raja Baba

A Message of Love from Jesus (Sananda) The purpose of this booklet is to extend ascension information beyond our New Age readership; produced by Oughten House

Please note: The above list constitutes only a partial listing of our literature, music, poems, children books, tapes, artwork, and other products. Let's keep in touch. Let us serve you.

BOOK GIFT CERTIFICATES
Treat your friend to a book.
It's a great surprise!

Book gift certificates offer a special 20% discount from the suggested retail price.

Catalogs will gladly be sent upon request. Book orders must be prepaid: check, money order, international coupon, VISA, MasterCard accepted. Include shipping and handling (US postal book rate): $3.50 first book; add 50¢ for each additional book. Send orders to:

OUGHTEN HOUSE PUBLICATIONS
P.O. Box 2008
Livermore • California • 94551-2008 • USA
Phone (510) 447-2332
FAX (510) 447-2376

READER NETWORKING AND MAILING LIST ✧✧✧

The ascension process presents itself as a new dimension and reality for many of us on Planet Earth. Oughten House Publications now stands in the midst of many Starseeds and Lightworkers who seek to know more. Thousands of people worldwide are reaching out to find others of like mind and to network with them.

You have the opportunity to stay informed and be on our networking mailing list. Send us the enclosed Information Reply Card or a letter. We will do our best to keep you and your network of friends up to date with ascension-related literature, materials, author tours, workshops, and channelings.

If you have a network or small mailing list you would like to share, please send it along.

NOTES

∽ NOTES ∽